MODERN HUMANITIES RESEARCH ASSOCIATION
LIBRARY OF MEDIEVAL WELSH LITERATURE
VOLUME 7

GENERAL EDITORS
ANN PARRY OWEN
ERICH POPPE
SIMON RODWAY

CHILDREN AND PARENTS
IN MEDIEVAL WELSH LAW

MODERN HUMANITIES RESEARCH ASSOCIATION
LIBRARY OF MEDIEVAL WELSH LITERATURE

ALREADY PUBLISHED

Early Welsh Gnomic and Nature Poetry
Edited by Nicolas Jacobs (2012)

Historical Texts from Medieval Wales
Edited by Patricia Williams (2012)

A Selection of Early Welsh Saga Poems
Edited by Jenny Rowland (2014)

Arthur in Early Welsh Poetry
Edited by Nerys Ann Jones (2019)

*Hystoria Gweryddon yr Almaen: The Middle Welsh Life of
St Ursula and the 11,000 Virgins*
Edited by Jane Cartwright (2020)

Delw y Byd: A Medieval Welsh Encyclopedia
Edited by Natalia I. Petrovskaia (2020)

To sign up to the series mailing list, email lmwl@mhra.org.uk

www.texts.mhra.org.uk

CHILDREN AND PARENTS IN MEDIEVAL WELSH LAW

EDITED BY

SARA ELIN ROBERTS

MODERN HUMANITIES RESEARCH ASSOCIATION
Library of Medieval Welsh Literature 7
2025

Published by
The Modern Humanities Research Association
Salisbury House
Station Road
Cambridge CB1 2LA
United Kingdom

© Modern Humanities Research Association, 2025

Sara Elin Roberts has asserted her right under the Copyright, Designs and Patents Act 1988 to be identified as the author of this work. Parts of this work may be reproduced as permitted under legal provisions for fair dealing (or fair use) for the purposes of research, private study, criticism, or review, or when a relevant collective licensing agreement is in place. All other reproduction requires the written permission of the copyright holder who may be contacted at rights@mhra.org.uk.

First published 2025

ISBN 978-1-83954-559-7 (hardback)
ISBN 978-1-83954-560-3 (paperback)

Typeset in Minion Pro by Allset Journals & Books, Scarborough, UK

CONTENTS

Preface	ix
Abbreviations: References	xi
Abbreviations: Grammatical	xiii
Abbreviations: Welsh Law Manuscripts	xiv
Introduction	1
Medieval Welsh Law	1
The Welsh Law Manuscripts	3
The Lawtexts	5
Society and the Kindred in the Laws	7
The Text: Children and Parents	9
The Manuscript: 'Llyfr Gruffudd ap Nicolas'	18
Editorial Methodology	20
General observations	20
Language and orthography	23
Spelling system	24
Mutations	25
Common constructions and forms	26
Chapter numbering and presentation	27
Text	29
Notes	34
Glossary	87
Bibliography	102

*I'm plant
a'm rhieni*

PREFACE

Cyfraith Hywel, the law of Medieval Wales, is a huge subject area and one which has a reputation for being difficult. The texts are often long, with parts written in complex technical Middle Welsh and including terminology which is extremely specific and not encountered elsewhere. Some parts of the laws can be rather heavy going. The aim of this text is to provide a starting point for reading and studying the laws, and so this volume presents a relatively short but complete text on a topic concerning family life: children and parents. The Introduction gives the background and context to the subject of Cyfraith Hywel, and the same for the text in question, the discussion avoiding going into complex and detailed textual examination. Information is presented on a need-to-know basis, giving enough to enable the reader to understand the context of this text within the law as a whole, but hopefully without causing utter dejection before reaching the text itself. The bibliography and the references point the reader to further reading which gets to grips with the textual history and provides deeper discussions of the lawtexts and their relationships.

The subject of children and parents in the Middle Ages is also a big one, and the Welsh text has received less attention than its Irish counterpart. As the purpose of this book is to present a Middle Welsh reading text, the text is explained in the Introduction and analysed in detail in the Notes, but it is examined as a standalone text and only passing reference is made to works on the wider European context of the history of children and parents in the Middle Ages. It should be noted that there are very important parallels between this text and similar texts in Ireland, and brief reference is made to the broader and comparative context.

In preparing this text, I am indebted to several scholars who have helped me and contributed in various ways to this work and to my work on Welsh law in general. Prof. Thomas Charles-Edwards, my DPhil supervisor, taught me to edit Medieval Welsh legal texts, and working on this text took me back to happy times in seminars and discussions with him at Oxford. I am also indebted to the members of Seminar Cyfraith Hywel and have benefitted from many discussions at the biannual meetings; the four editions produced by Seminar Cyfraith Hywel are models of detailed textual work on the Welsh laws. This work has been completed in the post-Repertory period, as it were. Receiving the beautiful volumes of the *Repertory of Welsh Manuscripts and Scribes* was an emotional moment, but this and all of my (and others') work on the Welsh lawtexts remains indebted to Daniel Huws. I would also like to thank Gruffudd Antur for his always valuable comments and discussions on manuscripts. People who have assisted me and answered various questions on Middle Welsh include Barry Lewis, Guto Rhys, Simon Rodway, and Ceridwen Lloyd-Morgan. Luke Blaidd was particularly helpful in discussing terminology and gender terms with me, and was generous in sharing his forthcoming work on the topic. Bringing this firmly into the twenty-first century, there are invaluable discussions and helpful people on the academic Facebook groups: Lahney Preston-Matto and Elizabeth Boyle in particular helped me in providing references and tracking down work. Cailix Lawrie tested the text and notes for me, and I am grateful to them for that. Particular gratitude goes to the three editors of the MHRA Library of Medieval Welsh Literature, Prof. Ann Parry Owen, Prof. Erich Poppe, and Dr Simon Rodway, for asking me to undertake this work, and for their extremely valuable insights and detailed comments on earlier drafts; I also thank them for their support and ready assistance. I am also grateful to the MHRA Publishing Manager, Simon Davies, who made the process smooth and efficient, and my wonderful and eagle-eyed copyeditor Puck Fletcher, for their thorough and professional work. It is an honour to be included in this important series, and I have benefitted greatly from the books already published in the Library of Medieval Welsh Literature. Naturally, any errors or omissions which remain are my own.

My main vote of gratitude goes to my family: my husband, Tim, has supported me in a very practical way by cooking supper, driving the children to after-school activities, and giving me the time to work on this text; he has also provided excellent cups of tea, and emotional support and encouragement, as well as reading through the text at various stages. Iestyn and Goronwy have been superb, getting on with other things while their mother is in the study, looking up words and reading manuscripts. I did this work knowing that they were behind me, supporting me. Diolch o galon i chi, fedra i ddim diolch digon!

ABBREVIATIONS: REFERENCES

AL   *Ancient Laws and Institutes of Wales*, ed. by Aneurin Owen, 2 vols (Public Records Commission, 1841). References are to Book number in capital Roman numerals, Chapter number in lowercase Roman numerals, and sentence number in Arabic numerals, e.g. VI.i.57. For Vol. I references are also given to the Code (VC, DC, GC): e.g. VC II.xvi.23.

DwC   *Damweiniau Colan*, ed. by Dafydd Jenkins (Cymdeithas Llyfrau Ceredigion, 1973). References are to numbered sentences.

GMW   *A Grammar of Middle Welsh*, ed. by D. Simon Evans (Dublin Institute for Advanced Studies, 1964). References are to numbered sections, denoted §, or to page numbers.

GPC   *Geiriadur Prifysgol Cymru: A Dictionary of the Welsh Language Online*, <https://www.geiriadur.ac.uk/gpc/gpc.html>

J(ed.)   *Cyfreithiau Hywel Dda yn ôl Llawysgrif Coleg yr Iesu LVII*, ed. by Melville Richards, 2nd edn (University of Wales Press, 1990). References are to page number and line number.

LAL   *Lawyers and Laymen: Studies in the History of Law Presented to Professor Dafydd Jenkins on his Seventy-Fifth Birthday, Gŵyl Ddewi 1986*, ed. by T. M. Charles-Edwards, Morfydd E. Owen, and Dafydd B. Walters (University of Wales Press, 1986)

LlBleg   *Llyfr Blegywryd*, ed. by Stephen J. Williams and J. Enoch Powell (University of Wales Press, 1942)

LlIor   *Llyfr Iorwerth: A Critical Text of the 'Venedotian Code' of Medieval Welsh Law*, ed. by Aled Rhys Wiliam (University of Wales Press, 1960). References are to numbered sections, denoted §, and sentence number, e.g. §98/4. References to page numbers refer to the notes or the introduction.

LT   *The Legal Triads of Medieval Wales*, ed. by Sara Elin Roberts (University of Wales Press, 2007). References are to triad number using the collection siglum and number, e.g. Q74, or to page numbers for the notes or introduction.

LTMW   *The Law of Hywel Dda: Law Texts from Medieval Wales*, ed. by Dafydd Jenkins (Gomer, 1986)

RWMS   *A Repertory of Welsh Manuscripts and Scribes, c.800–c.1800*, ed. by Daniel Huws (National Library of Wales, 2022)

TCC   *Tair Colofn Cyfraith. The Three Columns of Law in Medieval Wales: Homicide, Theft and Fire*, ed. by T. M. Charles-Edwards and Paul Russell, Welsh Legal History Society, 5 (Welsh Legal History Society,

2005). References are to numbered sections, denoted §, and sentence number.

WKC *The Welsh King and his Court*, ed. by T. M. Charles-Edwards, Morfydd E. Owen, and Paul Russell (University of Wales Press, 2000)

WLW *The Welsh Law of Women*, ed. by Dafydd Jenkins and Morfydd E. Owen (University of Wales Press, 1980)

ABBREVIATIONS: GRAMMATICAL

adj.	adjective	MW	Middle Welsh
adv.	adverb	n.	noun
advl	adverbial	neg.	negative
aff.	affixed	num.	numeral
affirm.	affirmative	obj.	object
art.	article	ord.	ordinal (numeral)
comp.	comparative	part.	particle
cond.	conditional	past	past tense
conj.	conjunction	pers.	personal
conjv.	conjunctive	pl.	plural
def.	definite	plupf.	pluperfect
dem.	demonstrative	poss.	possessive
f.	feminine	pref.	prefixed
1	first-person	prep.	preposition
fut.	future	pres.	present
habit.	habitual (consuetudinal)	pret.	preterite
imper.	imperative	pron.	pronoun
impf.	imperfect	pvbl	preverbal
imps.	impersonal	refl.	reflexive
ind.	indicative	rel.	relative
indep.	independent	sing.	singular
inf.	infixed	spv.	superlative
interr.	interrogative	3	third-person
lit.	literally	vb	verb
m.	masculine	vbl	verbal
ModW	Modern Welsh	v.n.	verb noun

ABBREVIATIONS: WELSH LAW MANUSCRIPTS

A	Aberystwyth, National Library of Wales, Peniarth MS 29
An	Aberystwyth, National Library of Wales, Peniarth MS 166
As	Aberystwyth, National Library of Wales, Peniarth MS 34
B	London, British Library, Cotton MS Titus D III
Bost	Aberystwyth, National Library of Wales, NLW MS 24029A
C	London, British Library, Cotton MS Caligula A III
Col	Aberystwyth, National Library of Wales, Peniarth MS 30
Crd	Cardiff Central Library, MS 2.7
D	Aberystwyth, National Library of Wales, Peniarth MS 32
E	London, British Library, Add. MS 14,931
Ep	Aberystwyth, National Library of Wales, Peniarth MS 258
F	Aberystwyth, National Library of Wales, Peniarth MS 34
G	Aberystwyth, National Library of Wales, Peniarth MS 35
H	Aberystwyth, National Library of Wales, Peniarth MS 164
I	Aberystwyth, National Library of Wales, Peniarth MS 38
J	Oxford, Jesus College, MS 57
K	Aberystwyth, National Library of Wales, Peniarth MS 40
L	London, British Library, Cotton MS Titus D IX
Lew	Aberystwyth, National Library of Wales, Peniarth MS 39
Llan	Aberystwyth, National Library of Wales, Llanstephan MS 29
M	Aberystwyth, National Library of Wales, Peniarth MS 33
Mk	Anglesey, MS in private collection at Bodorgan Hall
Mor	Aberystwyth, National Library of Wales, Peniarth MS 36C
N	Aberystwyth, National Library of Wales, Peniarth MS 36B
O	Aberystwyth, National Library of Wales, Peniarth MS 36A
P	Aberystwyth, National Library of Wales, Peniarth MS 259A
Q	Aberystwyth, National Library of Wales, Wynnstay MS 36
R	Aberystwyth, National Library of Wales, Peniarth MS 31
S	London, British Library, Add. MS 22,356
T	London, British Library, Harley MS 958
Tim	Aberystwyth, National Library of Wales, Llanstephan MS 116
Tr	Cambridge, Trinity College, MS 1329
U	Aberystwyth, National Library of Wales, Peniarth MS 37
V	London, British Library, Harley MS 4353
W	London, British Library, Cotton MS Cleopatra A XIV
X	London, British Library, Cotton MS Cleopatra B V

Y	Aberystwyth, National Library of Wales, NLW MS 20143A
Z	Aberystwyth, National Library of Wales, Peniarth MS 259B

Latin Manuscripts

Latin A	Aberystwyth, National Library of Wales, Peniarth MS 28
Latin B	London, British Library, Cotton MS Vespasian E XI
Latin C	London, British Library, Harley MS 1796
Latin D	Oxford, Bodleian Library, MS Rawlinson C. 821
Latin E	Cambridge, Corpus Christi College, MS 454

INTRODUCTION

Medieval Welsh Law

Cyfraith Hywel, the law of medieval Wales, existed as a legal system current in Wales and applicable to people in all parts of Wales until it was abolished by the Acts of Union in 1536. Wales in the Middle Ages was not a unified country; it was formed of a number of territories, each with its own ruler, and the shape of those territories varied according to circumstances and at different points in time. However, some aspects gave Wales its own identity, and these included the language, and Cyfraith Hywel. The law described the Welsh as a single people, separate and distinct from others, and it also gave a sense of unity as the Welsh could be identified as people who were subject to this law.[1] The law of medieval Wales was a home-grown system, different to the common law in England, and also different to the law of the church, canon law. It has some similarity to Irish law, and it also borrows concepts from other legal systems — traces of Roman law can be seen, as well as later texts which are based on English actions[2] — but Cyfraith Hywel was created in Wales, by the lawyers and for the lawyers.

The law is attributed to Hywel ap Cadell, also known as Hywel Dda (d. 950). This attribution is found in the prologues to the law manuscripts, where a description is given of Hywel, king of all Wales, calling an assembly in Whitland to examine the laws.[3] The prologues to the law manuscripts are the only evidence for Hywel's legal activity, and while such a prologue is found in the earliest surviving law manuscripts, the earliest manuscripts date from c. 1250, some three hundred years after Hywel's death. However, the extant Welsh law manuscripts are copies of earlier texts which are no longer in existence. Hywel Dda was a ruler of a large part of Wales in the tenth century, a period for which there is very little evidence in general, but Hywel was well established as a ruler and had a stable reign, which provided the circumstances for the flourishing of culture, including law. There is no evidence for any

---

[1] R. R. Davies, 'Law and National Identity in Thirteenth-Century Wales', in *Welsh Society and Nationhood: Historical Essays Presented to Glanmor Williams*, ed. by R. R. Davies (University of Wales Press, 1984), pp. 51–69 (p. 53).
[2] Dafydd Jenkins, 'The Significance of the Law of Hywel', *Transactions of the Honourable Society of the Cymmrodorion*, 1977, pp. 54–76 (p. 63).
[3] T. M. Charles-Edwards, *Wales and the Britons, 350–1074* (Oxford University Press, 2012), p. 270; Huw Pryce, 'The Prologues to the Welsh Lawbooks', *Bulletin of the Board of Celtic Studies*, 33 (1986), pp. 151–82 (p. 166).

cultural activity during his time, but he was a regular visitor at the court of Athelstan of Mercia, 'King of the English' from 927 to 939 and a known lawmaker, and Hywel may have been influenced by him.[4] Whether Hywel undertook any legal activity in Wales — or whether any happened under his blessing — cannot be proved, but it cannot be disproved either, and the lawtexts' attribution may be based on some historical fact which can no longer be verified.[5]

Cyfraith Hywel certainly has an early origin and may even have started to develop as early as the post-Roman period. The earliest surviving law manuscripts date from the mid-thirteenth century, but no Welsh manuscript of any type has survived from before that time. The law in the manuscripts is difficult to date precisely since the lawbooks developed and evolved over time, so the law in them does not belong to one specific point in history. Indeed, the prologues do not claim that Hywel Dda himself created the law at his assembly in Whitland; there is an acknowledgement that there was already law in Wales before his time, which Hywel and the learned men examined and revised, keeping the good parts. The lawtexts contain different layers of texts from different periods, and some of these texts are early, before Hywel's time.[6] The earliest surviving lawtexts, which date from the mid-thirteenth century, are copies of earlier exemplars, and at least some parts of the law can be dated to the twelfth century or earlier and have a pre-Norman origin.[7] There are also two surviving legal texts in Old Welsh, which show that legal texts were being recorded in Welsh at an early date; this may suggest an earlier origin for the Welsh lawtexts than the thirteenth century.[8]

The lawtexts therefore do not give an accurate picture of Welsh society at a particular point in time, although some parts of the laws may be roughly datable, in particular the sections which were made in Gwynedd in the mid-thirteenth century, where there was a flourishing of cultural activity.[9] The law

---

[4] *LTMW*, pp. xi-xvi; Kari Maund, *The Welsh Kings: The Medieval Rulers of Wales* (Tempus, 2000), p. 48. Charles-Edwards discusses two schools of thought on Hywel Dda and the laws: either to accept the attribution, or to see 'the attribution as belonging to a wider European pattern by which lawbooks of the twelfth and thirteenth centuries were attributed to authoritative figures of the past'. Charles-Edwards, *Wales and the Britons*, p. 268.

[5] Pryce, 'Prologues', p. 166. See also Charles-Edwards, *Wales and the Britons*, p. 268.

[6] See for example the text known as the 'Seven Bishop-Houses of Dyfed', which may be dated to the second half of the ninth century or the beginning of the tenth. T. M. Charles-Edwards, 'The Seven Bishop-Houses of Dyfed', *Bulletin of the Board of Celtic Studies*, 24.3 (1970-72), pp. 247-62 (pp. 248-49).

[7] T. M. Charles-Edwards, *The Welsh Laws* (Writers of Wales) (University of Wales Press, 1989), pp. 70-74.

[8] Dafydd Jenkins, *Cyfraith Hywel: Rhagarweiniad i Gyfraith Gynhenid Cymru'r Oesau Canol* (Gomer, 1970), pp. 3, 9; Sara Elin Roberts, *The Growth of Law in Medieval Wales, c.1100-c.1500* (The Boydell Press, 2022), pp. 7-9.

[9] Roberts, *Growth of Law*, p. 8, and see also pp. 67-68.

continued in use throughout the Middle Ages, and the development of the law after the conquest of Wales in 1282 can be traced to south Wales and the March, the borderlands of England and Wales.

The Welsh Law Manuscripts

Cyfraith Hywel is a subject well represented in manuscripts. There are over forty manuscripts containing a text of Cyfraith Hywel, a high number for any genre, and these are all relatively lengthy texts. They present the law in sophisticated, technical Middle Welsh, and the high number of manuscripts of Cyfraith Hywel, from throughout the Middle Ages, is testament to the importance and significance of the law.

The manuscripts are known by letter-names, or 'sigla'. Many of these were assigned by Aneurin Owen in his 1841 edition of the laws, but since there are more manuscripts than there are letters of the alphabet, several of the manuscripts have two- or three-letter abbreviations.[10] Most of the Welsh law manuscripts are unique in some way — very few are direct copies of other extant manuscripts — but most of them can be grouped into redactions, as the texts show similarity in organization and contain the same material as other extant manuscripts of Welsh law. Having said that, some manuscripts do not fit into any group. The five Latin manuscripts form their own group, largely because they are in Latin, but their texts are generally not very similar. The Welsh-language manuscripts are organized into three groups, named after pre-eminent lawyers referenced in the preface to each group (Cyfnerth, Blegywryd, Iorwerth).

The Cyfnerth redaction manuscripts contain the earliest version of the laws, although six of the seven manuscripts in this redaction date to the fourteenth century.[11] The manuscripts form a rather loose group, and while the same sections of law occur in the Cyfnerth manuscripts, with similar wording, it is a complex group which does not work as neatly as the other redactions. The Cyfnerth texts are the shortest texts and may show the early development of the laws.

By far the largest group in terms of the number of manuscripts as well as the length of many of the manuscripts it contains, the Blegywryd redaction has eighteen manuscripts.[12] Five date from the first half of the fourteenth century, and four from the mid-fourteenth century. The remainder are from the late

---

[10] Roberts, *Growth of Law*, p. 11, and see the complete list in that work on pp. xv–xvii.

[11] The manuscripts in this group are U, V, W, X, Z, Mk, and the Laws of Court from Y; Roberts, *Growth of Law*, pp. 16–18. One of the manuscripts, Z (NLW, Peniarth MS 259B), is a sixteenth-century copy of a lost fourteenth-century text.

[12] They are I, J, L, M, N, O, P, Q, R, S, T, Crd, Bost, Ep, Llan, Tim, Tr, and the second part of Y; Roberts, *Growth of Law*, pp. 14–16.

fourteenth to the mid-fifteenth centuries, and four of these later manuscripts are direct copies of other manuscripts in the group.[13] While the Blegywryd manuscripts are fourteenth- and fifteenth-century in date, parts of the texts are considerably older. The Blegywryd redaction as a whole is a translation of a Latin text, similar to the extant Latin D manuscript, and this shows that parts of the Blegywryd redaction date back to *c.* 1300. Several of the Blegywryd texts are very lengthy and show considerable development. They were based on a number of exemplars which were copied in addition to the Blegywryd exemplar that formed the basis of the text. Among these exemplars there were practitioners' workbooks, sections of texts circulating locally, and a Iorwerth-type text circulating in south Wales, parts of which were copied into several manuscripts in the Blegywryd redaction.

The earliest law manuscripts in Welsh are found among the eight manuscripts in the Iorwerth redaction.[14] Five of the Iorwerth group date to the thirteenth century, and a sixth is dated to *c.* 1404. The other two are from the mid-fifteenth century. The text contained in the Iorwerth manuscripts can be dated to the thirteenth century — close in date to that of the earliest manuscripts in the group — and it reflects legal activity undertaken in Gwynedd during the time of Llywelyn ab Iorwerth. Some of the work is attributed to a jurist called Iorwerth ap Madog (fl. ?1240–?1268), and he may have reorganized the Iorwerth manuscripts into a tripartite structure, as well as compiling or even creating some sections himself.[15] The Iorwerth manuscripts are fairly uniform in order and content and form a close group.

Other Welsh law manuscripts defy categorization as they do not have enough of a redaction text to fit neatly into one of the other groups of Welsh redactions.[16] For example, Col, National Library of Wales (NLW), Peniarth MS 30, is linked to the Iorwerth redaction and seems to be a revised version of it. Three of the non-redaction manuscripts form a subgroup linked to north-east Wales, and contain material which might be of use to a legal practitioner, including a collection of model pleadings.[17] This is a feature of these manuscripts, and they include material selectively, because they have a use for it, rather than systematically copying a redaction text. With the exception of Col, they are later texts, dating from the late fourteenth to the fifteenth centuries.

---

[13] Crd is a direct copy of L; M is a copy of Bost; and both Ep and P are copies of Q.
[14] Manuscripts A, B, C, D, E, G, K, and Lew; Roberts, *Growth of Law*, pp. 11–14.
[15] Roberts, *Growth of Law*, pp. 67–72.
[16] These include An, As, Col, F, H and Mor; Roberts, *Growth of Law*, pp. 18–20.
[17] Roberts, *Growth of Law*, pp. 199–204.

The Lawtexts

Cyfraith Hywel was a codified system of law. Codification is the process whereby the law and legal rules are collected together and presented as a code, a 'codex' or book of law. Legal codes are often organized by subject, and this is the case with the Cyfraith Hywel books, which can be subdivided into different topics, called tractates. The aim of the lawbooks was to discuss all of the law of Wales, and the tractates of Welsh law cover a large variety of subjects. Most of the complete lawbooks open with a Prologue, an introductory section which describes how Hywel ap Cadell gathered together the wisest men from across Wales to examine the laws.[18] The Prologues may have been composed to give the Welsh laws imagined royal and ecclesiastical origins — as is the case with other European legal texts — and as discussed above, it is not possible to prove the veracity of the link between the laws and Hywel ap Cadell.[19] The Prologue is often followed by the Laws of Court (*Cyfraith Llys*), a lengthy section discussing the royal court, listing the officers who served the king and detailing their privileges and duties.[20] This may have been outdated by the thirteenth century — indeed, it is often absent from later legal compilations — but again emphasized the royal links of the Welsh lawbooks.[21]

The Laws of Court is seen as one of the main subdivisions of the lawbooks: it is the first of three in the Iorwerth manuscripts which follow a tripartite structure, and is described as the first of three main parts in the Blegywryd manuscripts too.[22] In both Iorwerth and Blegywryd, the Laws of Country (*Cyfraith y Wlad*) is a second large section, comprised of smaller texts on a variety of subjects.[23] These include *Tair Colofn Cyfraith* ('the Three Columns of Law'), on *galanas* ('homicide'), theft, and arson, as well as linked sections on witnesses, such as *Y Naw Tafodiog* ('the Nine Tongued-Ones'); the value of limbs; and sections detailing the *galanas* and *sarhaed* compensation payments.[24] Other major topics covered in the Laws of Country include Suretyship and Contract (*Mechniaeth*); Land Law (*Cyfraith Tir*); and the Law of Women (*Cyfraith y Gwragedd*). The Blegywryd manuscripts also include the Value

---

[18] For an example see *LTMW*, p. 1.
[19] *LTMW*, p. xiii; Pryce, 'Prologues', p. 166.
[20] *WKC*, p. 3.
[21] Roberts, *Growth of Law*, p. 63.
[22] Roberts, *Growth of Law*, pp. 139–40.
[23] There is no formal statement in the Cyfnerth manuscripts which describes a tripartite structure, but the ending of the Laws of Court and the start of the Laws of Country are marked in those manuscripts, as they are in the Blegywryd manuscripts. See A. W. Wade-Evans, *Welsh Medieval Law, Being a Text of the Laws of Howel the Good* (Oxford University Press, 1909; repr. Scientia Verlag Aalen, 1979), pp. 36–37; Sara Elin Roberts, *Llawysgrif Pomffred: An Edition and Study of Peniarth MS 259B* (Brill, 2011), pp. 90–93; J(ed.), p. 23.
[24] Charles-Edwards, *Welsh Laws*, pp. 27–28; on *Tair Colofn Cyfraith* see *TCC*.

of Wild and Tame (*Gwerth Gwyllt a Dof*) in this category, along with Corn Damage (*Llwgr Ŷd*), and lists of values of equipment; in the Iorwerth manuscripts these, along with *Tair Colofn Cyfraith*, have been moved to the Test Book (*Llyfr Prawf*). However, the Iorwerth manuscripts have sections in the Laws of Country which are not found in the other redactions: these may be 'new' compositions made in Gwynedd in the thirteenth century, and they include a section on Church Protection, a sophisticated tractate on Injury to Animals, and a lengthy discussion on children and parents, which is the subject of this volume.[25] I will refer to the section as Children and Parents although it has no title in the manuscripts.

The third section in the Blegywryd manuscripts is said to be *Arferion Cyfraith* ('Practices of Law'),[26] and in Iorwerth the third section is the Test Book, said to have been compiled by Iorwerth ap Madog in thirteenth-century Gwynedd.[27] Iorwerth ap Madog appears to have reorganized the texts, moving sections which were found in the Laws of Country in earlier texts to create his practitioners' handbook, the Test Book, consisting of the sections which the justice needed to know in order to practice law.[28] The Test Book comprises *Tair Colofn Cyfraith*, discussing homicide, theft, and arson; the Value of Wild and Tame, giving a compensation value for animals 'which man may use' and describing their characteristics; lists of values of houses and equipment; *Cyfar*, a section detailing how to carry out joint ploughing; and Corn Damage, on the process to follow when another man's animals damage crops in the field.[29]

Some of the sections in the Iorwerth Test Book are found in the Laws of Country in Blegywryd and Cyfnerth, and this may preserve the original organization. These sections were revised and moved to the Test Book, and there is no reason to doubt that this was the work of Iorwerth ap Madog himself.[30] Corn Damage was a recognizable section and is found in Cyfnerth and Blegywryd as well as in the Latin texts, but it appears that it was rewritten in a new format for the Iorwerth Test Book.[31] There is no tractate on *Cyfar* ('joint ploughing') in Cyfnerth and Blegywryd, although a single sentence in Cyfnerth suggests that the concept was known.[32] The sophisticated *Cyfar* tractate may have been composed for the Iorwerth Test Book, perhaps as a summary of local practice or custom, if not created from scratch.

Iorwerth ap Madog's work on the Test Book is acknowledged, but he may

---

[25] Charles-Edwards, *Welsh Laws*, pp. 27–28.
[26] Roberts, *Growth of Law*, pp. 133–59.
[27] Charles-Edwards, *Welsh Laws*, pp. 29–31; Roberts, *Growth of Law*, pp. 67–72.
[28] Charles-Edwards, *Welsh Laws*, p. 30.
[29] Charles-Edwards, *Welsh Laws*, p. 28; see also *LTMW*, pp. 141–209; and *LlIor*, §§104–60.
[30] Roberts, *Growth of Law*, p. 67.
[31] Roberts, *Growth of Law*, pp. 68–72.
[32] Roberts, *Growth of Law*, p. 69.

have also worked on other parts of the Iorwerth text: indeed, if sections were being moved around, then he would have had a thorough understanding of the entire Laws of Country. There are tractates within the Laws of Country in Iorwerth which are not found in Cyfnerth and Blegywryd, and these may be 'new' compositions made at the same time that the Iorwerth Test Book was compiled and sections were being revised for that part. These include discussions on Church Protection and a section on Injury to Animals, another highly sophisticated section, elegantly written and drawing on Roman and European legal traditions. The text on Children and Parents is also a 'new' section which is only found written in full as a tractate in the Iorwerth texts; Robin Chapman Stacey notes that it is 'a deliberate addition'.[33] Some parts of the tractate are found in the Blegywryd texts, but it is not written as an orderly section there: the concepts and rules are largely found in the Law of Women in Blegywryd. In Iorwerth, however, the tractate is neat and organized, and it follows a logical structure for the most part.

Within the section, there are several references which show that this is a self-consciously written text: there are references to earlier discussions, for example, *E deu uab rydywedassam ny uchot* ('the two sons we named above'), to avoid repeating things which have already been discussed in full. This suggests that the tractate had a written tradition, perhaps predating the form in the earliest Iorwerth manuscripts, but the extant text is a final version. There is also reference in the text to a well-known triad,[34] *Tri dyngoll cenedl* ('The three dire losses of a kindred'), found in all of the redactions at different points. In Blegywryd the triad is found in discussions of homicide in the *Tair Colofn Cyfraith* tractate, a section which was revised for the Iorwerth Test Book.[35] The *Tri dyngoll* section in Iorwerth seems to have been rewritten from a triad, again suggesting heavy editorial or even rewriting work on the section.[36]

Society and the Kindred in the Laws

As has been noted, Cyfraith Hywel was a legal system created by lawyers and for lawyers. This was a sophisticated and flexible system: it was designed to operate at a local level, and would work without an enforcing royal structure (but would equally work if there was such a structure in place). The political organization of medieval Wales — which did not have a unified territory under

---

[33] Robin Chapman Stacey, *Law and the Imagination in Medieval Wales* (University of Pennsylvania Press, 2018), p. 175, and see also n. 129.
[34] Triads are sentences listing legal concepts in groups of three, and they occur in lengthy collections in the law manuscripts; for a full study see LT.
[35] Sara Elin Roberts, '*Tri Dygyngoll Cenedl*: The Development of a Triad', *Studia Celtica*, 37 (2003), pp. 163–82 (p. 167).
[36] Roberts, '*Tri Dygyngoll Cenedl*', pp. 169–70, 173.

a strong ruler for much of its history — may explain the lack of punishment in the law: this is not a moral code. Rather, the emphasis throughout the law is on mutual responsibility: people had to take responsibility for their own actions, and pay compensation for any injury or loss caused to others. Every person had a life-value, known as *galanas*, which was calculated according to their status and paid to their family if they were killed by another. All injuries had to be paid for, and there are lists of the values of parts of the body, as well as values for specific injuries — bruises, blood loss, blows, hair pulling — which were to be paid if caused by another.[37] A distinction was made between accidental injuries, which had to be compensated, and deliberate injuries, where there was an additional payment — *sarhaed* (lit. 'insult'), calculated as a proportion of the person's *galanas* value.[38]

Enforcing the law in medieval Wales did not lie with the ruler — again, due to the political organization — but it operated on a local level to a great extent. The law depended on mutual responsibility and an element of trust, but it also worked on the expectation that the society was organized as small, local units where everybody knew each other. The figures of authority in these local areas were not necessarily appointed by the Crown or a ruling figure, but were men of importance on a local level, or, more specifically, within a family group, the *cenedl* ('kindred'). The *pencenedl* ('head of kindred') had authority over the kindred, and his role could be very similar to that of the king.[39] Other senior members of local society could also have some authority, or are mentioned in the laws. There are references in the laws to *hynafgwyr* ('oldest men'), although Jenkins states that 'this expression does not seem to imply any official status'.[40] *Goreugwyr* (lit. 'the best men' from the kindred), however, may have had some special status. Belonging to a kindred was crucial for any man, as it was the basis for his status and had a bearing on paying and receiving the *galanas* fine.[41]

In many cases, it would be clear at birth to which kindred any male child would belong and there would be no discussion. This assumes that the child's father is known, however, and the law spends a considerable amount of time discussing sons of unknown fathers. This would be a son born to a woman who had kept her relationship secret — a *gwraig llwyn a pherth* ('woman of bush and brake').[42] Once the woman had given birth to a son, he needed to be linked

---

[37] See *LTMW*, pp. xxx–xxxi; Sara Elin Roberts, '"By the Authority of the Devil": The Operation of Welsh and English Law in Medieval Wales', in *Authority and Subjugation in the Writing of Medieval Wales*, ed. by Simon Meecham-Jones and Ruth Kennedy (Palgrave Macmillan, 2008), pp. 85–97 (p. 87).

[38] Roberts, '"By the Authority of the Devil"', p. 87.

[39] T. M. Charles-Edwards, *Early Irish and Welsh Kinship* (Oxford University Press, 1993), pp. 201–11.

[40] *LTMW*, p. 277.

[41] Charles-Edwards, *Kinship*, pp. 181–200.

[42] Sara Elin Roberts and Ceridwen Lloyd-Morgan, 'In the Undergrowth: Llwyn a Pherth and

to a man, which would mean that he had a kindred; it was only in exceptional circumstances that a son would belong to his mother's kindred.[43] The process of affiliation to a kindred was important, and a formal procedure is set out in all of the redactions: in triads in Cyfnerth and Blegywryd, but as part of the tractate on Children and Parents in the Iorwerth texts. There is also a mirroring procedure for denying a son from a kindred, but it is clear from the text here that denial would become an option only after the mother had attempted to affiliate a son to a father; a son born into the kindred from an acknowledged relationship could not be denied. The process is for sons of doubtful paternity. If the father has acknowledged the son — by giving goods to rear him — he cannot then deny him. Meanwhile, a mother has only one opportunity to affiliate a son to a father: she must select the man she assumes is the father, and if that man denies that he is the father, there is no other opportunity. She may not choose several candidates for her son's father. Many of the provisions in the lengthy section in Iorwerth discuss situations where a son may not be denied, such as an attempt to abuse the system by denying a son who has committed an offence in order to avoid taking responsibility for compensation with the resultant financial loss. The process is not permitted to be used for financial gain (or loss), and much weight is put on acknowledging a son early on, since an acknowledged son — even if the formal process has not been followed — cannot be denied once he has started to be problematic in the kindred.

The Text: Children and Parents

The text presented here is from three different sources, but all found in one manuscript, siglum Q (NLW, Wynnstay MS 36), and it brings together several discussions on the subject of children and parents in Cyfraith Hywel. The first section is from the Blegywryd redaction, and this is followed by the tractate from the Iorwerth tradition. Unlike several of the Iorwerth tractates, this one does not have a title in the manuscripts. Dafydd Jenkins, in his translation of the Iorwerth text, labelled this tractate 'Family Law', the ninth section in his Laws of Country.[44] He gave no explanation for the title, although family law is a well-known division of modern law. The subject under discussion in Cyfraith

---

Sexual Deviancy in Medieval Wales', in *Women's Literary Cultures in the Global Middle Ages: Speaking Internationally*, ed. by Kathryn Loveridge, Liz Herbert McAvoy, Sue Niebrzydowski, and Vicki Kay Price (D. S. Brewer, 2022), pp. 261–75; Sara Elin Roberts, 'Bells, Bulls, and Bushes: Secret Sex in the Laws', in *Cyfarwydd Mewn Cyfraith: Studies in Honour of Morfydd E. Owen*, ed. by Sara Elin Roberts, Simon Rodway, and Alexander Falileyev, Welsh Legal History Society, 17 (Welsh Legal History Society, 2022), pp. 112–23.
[43] Discussions on these situations are found in the text. See Text, §6.
[44] *LTMW*, p. 129.

Hywel is rather different, although 'Family' could be interpreted as referring to the kindred. Aled Rhys Wiliam did not apply titles to his edition, but in the conspectus this tractate was labelled 'Children'.[45] This is appropriate for the first part of the text, which opens with the foetus and discusses children, but the tractate goes on to discuss membership of the kindred and reaching adulthood. I will call the tractate Children and Parents, following the focus of the text in question. At the end of this edition, several *damweiniau* ('eventualities') from the large collections of *damweiniau* linked to the Iorwerth redaction have also been included.[46] There is some discussion in these texts on the early years of children, both male and, unusually, female, although the main focus is on legal provisions and rites of passage rather than on pleasant discussions about happy childhood. Similar discussions are found in other legal traditions, and it should be noted that there are parallels to several aspects of the texts presented here in Irish law.[47]

The Blegywryd text, §1, looks at rearing a child for the first two years of his life. This is found in the Law of Women in the Blegywryd manuscripts, near the beginning of that section, following rules on separation and the rights of women. It is followed by a discussion on women eloping secretly.[48] There is no equivalent section in the Cyfnerth manuscripts, but the text does occur in Latin in several of the Latin manuscripts, including Latin D.[49] The earliest Blegywryd manuscripts date from the first half of the fourteenth century;[50] however, the Blegywryd redaction is in large part a translation of a manuscript similar to Latin D,[51] and this section on rearing a child is found in Latin D, which dates from the second half of the thirteenth century, which means that the section is earlier than the first Welsh manuscripts containing it. The section is also in Latin B and Latin E, Latin B dating from the mid-thirteenth century.[52] The items listed in the Latin version are the same as the items found in the

---

[45] *LlIor*, p. xliv.
[46] *Damweiniau* are sentences taking the form 'If it happens that X, then Y'; see below, pp. 16–18. The word is not commonly translated.
[47] As a starting point, see Fergus Kelly, *A Guide to Early Irish Law* (Dublin Institute for Advanced Studies, 1988), pp. 81–91. The subject has been discussed in recent PhD dissertations and other published work. An overview of the bibliography can be found in Máirín Nic Eoin, 'From Childhood Vulnerability to Adolescent Delinquency: Literary Sources for the History of Childhood in Medieval Ireland', *Studia Hibernica*, 38 (2012), pp. 9–35.
[48] See *J(ed.)*, p. 61, l. 4–p. 65, l. 31, for the tractate, and p. 62, ll. 11–25, for this section.
[49] H. D. Emanuel, *The Latin Texts of the Welsh Laws* (University of Wales Press, 1967), p. 342, l. 29–p. 343, l. 3.
[50] See above, pp. 3–4; and see also Roberts, *Growth of Law*, pp. 14–15. Three are in the hand of the scribe Gwilym Wasta.
[51] Roberts, *Growth of Law*, pp. 14–15; and see H. D. Emanuel, 'The Book of Blegywryd and MS. Rawlinson 821', in *Celtic Law Papers*, ed. by D. Jenkins (Les Editions de la Librairie Encyclopédique, 1973), pp. 161–70.
[52] Emanuel, *Latin Texts*, p. 241, ll. 10–40 [Latin B]; p. 475, l. 29–p. 476, l. 8 [Latin E].

Blegywryd text of this section. This first part in Latin B, similar to the Blegywryd version, is the entire text in Latin E. The Latin texts have two words or phrases which are left in Welsh in the manuscripts: *dauat kyfhewin* (a sheep which is *cyfewin*, or *cyfoen*, 'a sheep big with lamb'),[53] and *gweren* ('a tallow cake'). This may indicate a Welsh origin for the Latin text, but the Blegywryd version came from the Latin, and the Latin text behind the Blegywryd redaction may well have derived from something similar to the text found in Latin B.

The section discusses the payment of goods to a woman who is rearing a child; the provisions for a son who is a villein are given first, and then a fuller list for the noble son. The items are divided between goods for the child and goods for the mother. Payments to the mother may be a surprising idea, as it would be assumed that a father would not be paying these items to the mother of his child in ordinary situations: the child would be reared within the family. There are two possible explanations for this: the payments listed may be the Welsh rules on fosterage, and the mother is the foster-mother; the alternative is that the mother and father are not together.[54] There is a suggestion that it may be the latter in the Latin texts, where the son is described as *clam adquiritur* ('secretly acquired (conceived)'): he is a *mab llwyn a pherth* ('son of bush and brake').[55] A son of doubted paternity would need to be provided for, by the father rather than by the mother, and this would be before the son was formally affiliated to the father. However, it must be remembered that giving goods for rearing a child in the Welsh laws is an admission of paternity, an acknowledgement of the son, so paying these goods to the mother would mean that the father would not be able to deny the son.[56] It is unclear why the Welsh text has omitted the reference to the son being a secret son — it makes little sense — but the section occurs directly before discussions in the Law of Women on secret marriages and elopement, the kinds of situations which might result in secret sons. It may be that the compiler of the texts wanted to keep the section, but decided for some reason to take out the reference to the secret son even though it makes the text less coherent.

The Blegywryd section focuses on payments for rearing a child, but it does reveal a little about the early years of a newborn baby, and the items that he might need. There are two parts to the text — the payments for rearing a villein, and a longer and more detailed section on rearing a noble son. The word order

---

[53] *GPC*, 'cyfewin²'.
[54] Of course, both could be the case: Anderson notes that fosterage may have been a convenient way of removing illegitimate royal children from the dangers posed by their half-brothers, as the illegitimate children would inherit land with the other brothers and could be seen as a threat. Katharine Anderson, '*Urth Noe e Tat*: The Question of Fosterage in High Medieval Wales', *North American Journal of Welsh Studies*, 4.1 (2004), pp. 1–11 (p. 10).
[55] See Roberts, 'Bells, Bulls, and Bushes'; and Roberts and Lloyd-Morgan, 'In the Undergrowth'.
[56] See Text, §7.8.

of the first sentence, with the note stating *a hynny a berthyn i'r taeogau* ('and that pertains to the villeins') at the end of the list, may point to editing work, adding an explanation to show the difference between the two sections: the payments for both sons are similar. The opening section of text (defective in Q) states *kyhyt ac y dyḃetpḃyt vry* ('as was stated above'), making it clear that this was a written text. It is less clear where the previous statement or discussion on rearing a noble son occurs: it does not appear to be in the Blegywryd texts, and there is nothing earlier on in the Law of Women which fits the subject.[57]

This text was written by someone who had hands-on experience of looking after a newborn baby, or at least reflects the realities of this task, since all of the items have a practical use: food and fuel for the breastfeeding mother and also for the infant; clothing for the mother (presumably so that she could breastfeed without stripping off, which could be cold) and swaddling for the son; and tallow, for lighting, since babies wake in the night. There are also valuable items: a sheep with her fleece and her lamb, which would have given the son a financial benefit but would also provide meat, as well as possibly milk, and wool for clothing and warmth; and the dairy cow with her calf for the mother, again, providing sellable animals or alternatively meat and dairy produce. The entire section is a rather lovely insight into rearing a newborn baby in medieval Wales, and it is more pleasant than the colder Iorwerth tractate.

In the Blegywryd Law of Women this text ends at this point, and the next section is on elopement; it is similar in Latin D. In Latin B, however, the remainder of the text is a few sentences discussing affiliation of children into a kindred, which is more similar to the Iorwerth tractate; the Iorwerth manuscripts may have used a text similar to this text (perhaps derived from the Latin manuscripts) as the basis for the extended section on Children and Parents.

The Iorwerth text on Children and Parents, sections §2–8 in this edition with numbered sentences for each section, is found in most of the Iorwerth manuscripts, but it is not in A (NLW, Peniarth MS 29), one of the mid-thirteenth-century manuscripts, as there is a hiatus in that manuscript at that point. It occurs in B, E, D, and K, and is also in Lew and G, but in both of those manuscripts it is incomplete due to missing leaves. It is also incomplete in C for the same reason: the text in C ends midway through what is §7.2 in this edition.

The text itself is found at the very end of the Laws of Country, immediately before the Test Book (attributed to Iorwerth ap Madog) in the Iorwerth manuscripts. It follows on from the section on the payments due from bond townships, with nothing to indicate a change of theme; it is not on the same topic as the preceding text. However, its location as the final subject in the Laws of Country is likely to be calculated: it ends the law with a discussion of the

---

[57] See Notes, 1.1.

family group and individual and collective or community responsibility. The section starts with the protection given to a foetus by the law and continues then through birth into life as part of a kindred, the bedrock unit of legal responsibility and enforcement of the law. This is not a 'royal' subject and little mention is made of the ruler or lord; the lawbooks open with the Laws of Court, emphasizing the royal links, but the Laws of Country closes with this section focusing on the family, a contrast, but also emphasizing the structure of society in the laws.[58] Children and Parents is a relatively orderly tractate, stand-alone, and may well have been composed around the time that Iorwerth ap Madog was editing the Iorwerth Test Book in the mid-thirteenth century. This is not material which would fit into the Test Book, according to the Test Book Preface, but it may well be part of Iorwerth ap Madog's re-editing of the Iorwerth redaction.

This tractate in Iorwerth brings together various rules on sons and daughters — with the main emphasis on sons — and the first three sections divide neatly and thematically, discussing the foetus, sons, and then daughters, including coming of age. This is a summary of the life-cycle according to Cyfraith Hywel.[59] The focus of the discussion is on legal stages and the change of status: there is no interesting detail on what children did, as that was not relevant for the lawyers. The opening section on the foetus is not found in the Cyfnerth or Blegywryd redactions, but there is a triad, *Tri gwerth cyfraith beichiogi gwraig* ('Three legal values of a woman's foetus'), on the compensation for damage to a foetus.[60] Morfydd Owen notes that 'most primitive law codes, both secular and canon, prescribe penalties for the death of the unborn child', and these are the rules in the Welsh laws.[61] However, there are differences between the wording of the triad and this section in Iorwerth: Owen notes that the Iorwerth text divides the pregnancy into three trimesters, and seems to be an early example of this. She notes that in the text the different stages of the foetus's growth are associated with colours, which is unusual, but the colours correspond to those described by Augustine and also Avicenna, in their writings. The Welsh text therefore 'may contain a conflation of the ancient teaching reported by Augustine and Avicenna with a trimester division'.[62] The triad from Cyfnerth and Blegywryd, as well as a discussion of the foetus in Latin A, are more likely to reflect earlier sources and 'orthodox medical doctrine' of the time.[63] T. M. Charles-Edwards notes that a baby would have had the status of

---

[58] Stacey, *Law and the Imagination*, p. 199.
[59] Charles-Edwards, *Kinship*, p. 175.
[60] *LT*, X39, Q26. In X, the triad is followed by the triad on denial and affiliation of a son.
[61] Morfydd E. Owen, 'Medics and Medicine', in *The Welsh King and his Court*, ed. by T. M. Charles-Edwards, Morfydd E. Owen, and Paul Russell (University of Wales Press, 2000), pp. 116–42 (p. 131).
[62] Owen, 'Medics and Medicine', p. 132.
[63] Owen, 'Medics and Medicine', pp. 131–32.

a foetus until they were named, and the Iorwerth text discusses this immediately after discussing the foetus; Charles-Edwards also notes that 'naming entails the public recognition of the sex of the baby', as well as of the child's kinship, since a boy would have a patronymic.[64]

Following on from the discussion of the foetus and the very early stage after childbirth, §3 turns to discuss sons, from birth until they come of age. This highlights the importance of male children, and the previous section, §2, also discusses male children exclusively after the initial opening on the foetus. The focus of the discussion is on the boy's legal status, although there is a difference: in §2, the son may swear his own oaths from the age of seven; in §3, there is no mention of this, but it states that his father is answerable for him. The son reaches full adulthood at fourteen, and Charles-Edwards notes that 'this is marked by the father taking his son to the lord and commending his son to him', but this is not feudal commendation as it is the father who presents the son to the lord; in feudalism the son would be doing it himself.[65] However, there is acknowledgement of the English practice in the sentence on becoming a knight: 'the foreign status of knighthood has been neatly assimilated to native categories. The *marchog* "knight" is only the *uchelwr* ['nobleman'] under a new name'.[66]

The section on sons is followed by a section on daughters, which follows the same pattern. It may have been intended to mirror the section on sons, but the main focus for the girl is on her childbearing years and payments which may be due. A girl is said in the text to reach puberty at twelve, and is then no longer dependent on her father. She may be given to a husband at that age, which Charles-Edwards takes to mean a betrothal, since she is not to have children until she is fourteen.[67] More details are given in the Law of Women on the rights of women and unmarried daughters, including marriage and offences against them: this section only discusses rites of passage and legal life-stages.

After discussing the life-cycle, there is a change in focus, and the text discusses membership of a kindred: how to affiliate children of doubted paternity into a kindred, and how to deny them, as well as various rules related to that topic. The main theme of this part is belonging to a kindred, something which was crucial in medieval Welsh law, since the inheritance of land was dependent on it; it also affected other things, such as the *galanas* payments.[68] In most cases it may be assumed that the son automatically enters into the kindred if he is the child of a marriage or union, but much of the focus here is on sons born secretly, or those whose fathers are less certain: this would include sons who

---

[64] Charles-Edwards, *Kinship*, pp. 175–76.
[65] Charles-Edwards, *Kinship*, p. 176.
[66] Charles-Edwards, *Kinship*, p. 176.
[67] Charles-Edwards, *Kinship*, p. 176.
[68] Charles-Edwards, *Kinship*, p. 201, and passim; and see above.

are *llwyn a pherth* ('of bush and brake').⁶⁹ There are also hints that children born to foreign fathers may have needed to be affiliated to a Welsh kindred because their Welsh lineage was not certain. In actual fact this part of the text does not necessarily fit with the neat sections on the foetus, sons, and then daughters, but it clearly brings together material on the subject of belonging to the kindred. The procedure for denying or accepting a son into a kindred is described in triads in Cyfnerth and Blegywryd and some of the Latin texts,⁷⁰ but there are very few triads in the Iorwerth redaction.⁷¹ The tractate is not one which is found in the Latin texts, or in the Cyfnerth or Blegywryd redaction, and the opening three sections are new material to a large extent. The tractate as a whole was presumably written especially for the Iorwerth text, possibly as part of Iorwerth ap Madog's editing work. As with the Test Book material, this tractate may have its origin in some material which is found in the other Welsh texts, or it may have developed material found in the Latin texts, perhaps starting from something similar to the text in Latin B, but extending it considerably.

The lengthy discussion on affiliation and denial starts at §5; it was all labelled 'Affiliation' by Dafydd Jenkins, but it was subdivided by Aled Rhys Wiliam.⁷² The length of this section and the various different rules, including the formal process of affiliation and denial, may be telling: children without automatic kindred membership may well have been a common occurrence. §5 opens by stating that if a son is to be denied from a kindred, he must first be affiliated (*dwyn*) following a particular legal procedure which is set out in two different scenarios. After this, the short procedure for denial is explained.

There is an interesting discussion in §6 on *Tri dygngoll cenedl* ('The three dire losses of a kindred').⁷³ It is a well-known piece of text, and it occurs as a triad in the Blegywryd, Cyfnerth, and Latin texts. A version of the triad also occurs in the Iorwerth redaction, although it does not have the traditional triad header. The text found here in Iorwerth seems to be an adapted version of the triad found in Cyfnerth and Blegywryd, perhaps taking into consideration the fact that the concept of *Tri dygngoll* was well known and using some of the ideas found in the triad in Blegywryd and Cyfnerth. The subject matter accords with the material in the preceding section, as it discusses special cases of denial and affiliation.

After the *Tri dygngoll cenedl* section and related to the subject of the triad,

---

⁶⁹ See Roberts, 'Bells, Bulls, and Bushes', p. 114.

⁷⁰ *LT*, pp. 60–63: X40 and variant in Mk46 and 47; see also Q185 and 186, and Y155.

⁷¹ See Sara Elin Roberts, 'The Iorwerth Triads', in *Tome: Studies in Medieval Celtic History and Law in Honour of Thomas Charles-Edwards*, ed. by Fiona Edmonds and Paul Russell (The Boydell Press, 2011), pp. 155–74 (p. 157).

⁷² *LTMW*, p. 132; *LlIor*, pp. 66–69, §§100–03.

⁷³ There is a detailed study of this text in Roberts, '*Tri Dygyngoll Cenedl*', pp. 163–82.

§7 has short sentences on different situations, all focused on affiliation or denial, particularly on the potential misuse of the process in order to gain from it. Rules state when someone is not permitted to deny another from a kindred. The difference in §7 seems to be that the son being affiliated is not an infant: he is perhaps of age, and so his mother is not taking the action to assign him as a newborn to his father. This is also the case in the denial process outlined in §6, where again the child is not an infant as there are instances where he has committed crimes: denial need not necessarily happen at birth. These sections are not reflected in the Blegywryd and Cyfnerth texts, which only discuss the affiliation or denial of a newborn child, and they may be later additions to the laws in Iorwerth, to reflect the changing society, or simply to broaden the scope of the law in terms of belonging to a kindred. The circumstances in which a child can be accepted into a kindred have been detailed earlier on in this tractate, in §4, but the focus in §8 is the ceremony of acceptance, emphasizing the role of the kindred. It gives the equivalent process to that for denial, already outlined. §8 is similar to the triads on affiliation and denial in Cyfnerth and Blegywryd, and the text in §8 has a tripartite structure. The tractate in Iorwerth comes to an end with §8, and, indeed, the Laws of Country in Iorwerth end at this point too, but the ending is not marked. In most of the Iorwerth manuscripts this final sentence of §8 is followed by the Test Book Preface.

The remainder of the text presented here is not a single unbroken passage of text, but *damweiniau* on the subject of children and parents taken from the large collection in manuscript Q. There is a Book of *Damweiniau* which follows immediately after the Iorwerth text in several of the Iorwerth manuscripts, and the collection also occurs in non-Iorwerth manuscripts.[74] Manuscript Q has a large collection of *damweiniau* which is similar to that in K, but the order and content of the collection is not the same as the *damweiniau* collections found in the other manuscripts.[75] Charles-Edwards discusses the purpose of the *damweiniau* and how they fit in with the Iorwerth text; it may be that the *damweiniau* collections were 'a way of incorporating Iorwerth concepts that were different from the material they already had': *damweiniau* collections may have included different Iorwerth material, or new material, without requiring a rewrite of the Iorwerth tractates.[76]

The six *damweiniau* gathered together in §9 are all on the same theme as the tractate on Children and Parents in Iorwerth, but there is no repetition of material here, and they each discuss unusual situations, or a development of

---

[74] For a discussion of *damweiniau*, see Roberts, *Growth of Law*, pp. 105–10.

[75] See Roberts, *Growth of Law*, p. 107; and Robin Chapman Stacey, 'Legal Writing in Medieval Wales: Damweiniau I', in *Wales and the Wider World: Welsh History in an International Context*, ed. by T. M. Charles-Edwards and R. J. W. Evans (Shaun Tyas, 2011), pp. 57–85 (p. 63, n. 27).

[76] Charles-Edwards, *Welsh Laws*, p. 53; Roberts, *Growth of Law*, p. 108.

the scenarios given in the Children and Parents tractate. The first discusses the legal position of an intersex person. This is not considered a problematic issue, but the laws set out their position on how to determine the status of the intersex person, as the male status is higher. This is done by allowing such a person to make their own choice to a great extent, and to choose how they identify. If they identify as both male and female, the higher status — male — is assigned to them, and they are entitled to patrimony. Provision is also made for any (male) children which the person may have, either by carrying the child themselves or by making another woman pregnant. This is the first modern edition of this particular *damwain*; it is included in *Ancient Laws and Institutes of Wales* (*AL*) but with a very insensitive Victorian English translation.

The next *damwain* from the collection discusses fosterage: the practice, which was known in Wales but is more familiar in Ireland, of sending a son to be reared by another family.[77] In her study of the subject, Llinos Beverley Smith notes that 'Fosterage is often cited as a significant feature of the medieval societies of the Celtic lands; but its contours are far more clearly identified in Ireland than they are in Wales', and she notes that the Welsh lawtexts refer only briefly to the practice: this is one of the main references in the laws.[78] However, evidence from other sources shows that fosterage was as common in medieval Wales as it was in Ireland, and Katharine Anderson states that

> there is certainly enough evidence to conclude that fosterage was being practiced in high medieval Wales. Although it may have developed from an early medieval tradition that was very close to the Irish model of fosterage, by the twelfth century the material for Wales suggests that a distinctive and much more limited kind of fosterage was being practiced.[79]

The focus of this *damwain* is once again on inheritance rights: according to this section the foster-son would receive all of his foster-father's goods if the foster-father had no other sons. However, it goes on to state that the foster-son would also receive a share of land along with his foster-brothers, as if he were one of them.[80] This gives serious implications to the practice of fosterage, and it also has a negative effect on the bondsman: his lord may give permission for a nobleman to give him his son to rear, and his rights to his own land (no doubt limited in the first place due to his social status) would pass to another man's son or be shared with his natural sons, which seems to be an abuse of power. Fosterage, however, may have served to 'lessen the social distance between orders and to familiarize the children of *uchelwyr* with the ways of the

---

[77] See Charles-Edwards, *Kinship*, p. 78; Llinos Beverley Smith, 'Fosterage, Adoption, and God-parenthood: Ritual and Fictive Kinship in Medieval Wales', *Welsh History Review*, 16.1 (1992), pp. 1–35.
[78] Smith, 'Fosterage, Adoption, and God-parenthood', p. 3.
[79] Anderson, '*Urth Noe e Tat*', pp. 10–11.
[80] Smith, 'Fosterage, Adoption, and God-parenthood', pp. 18–19.

bondman'.[81] There is another version of this text on fosterage, with similar wording (although not as a *damwain*), following the Land Law tractate in Iorwerth, in a section discussing royal rights to land.[82]

The following three *damweiniau* are found as a consecutive group. The *damweiniau* collections were sometimes organized by subject. These come under the loose subject-heading of children and parents: the first discusses twin boys and the implications of birth order to the inheritance of the family land. The youngest son had particular rights over the *tyddyn cyfreithiol* ('the legal toft'),[83] and was also responsible for making the division of the land. This is followed by a discussion on denying a girl from a kindred, which is a new situation not discussed elsewhere. It is unfortunate that very little detail is given on this exciting scenario, as the main discussion in the *damwain* is on who pays the girl's *amobr* (payable to the lord on marriage) and calculating the amount due, as it was generally subject to her father's status and his values. The third in the group changes the subject again and gives a precise definition of *mab dioddef* ('son by sufferance'), the concept which is discussed in the Children and Parents tractate in Iorwerth and which is contrasted with *mab deolef* ('son by clamour').

The last of the *damweiniau* in this selection discusses a mute woman and emphasizes the importance of being able to speak in law. There are cases in the law where a person may have a representative to speak on their behalf because the person is unable to speak in a way that is easily understood — they may have a speech impediment, or may not be able to speak Welsh.[84] Women were not permitted to speak in court, and they would have a *tafodiog* ('one with a tongue', a 'representative'), but in the case of affiliating or denying a child from a kindred, it seems that it had to be done by the woman's own mouth: they had to wait until the mother died. It is a strange provision, but it emphasizes the seriousness of the affiliation and denial processes.

The Manuscript: 'Llyfr Gruffudd ap Nicolas'

The text in this edition has been taken from Q (NLW, Wynnstay MS 36), a remarkable fifteenth-century manuscript of Welsh law now known as 'Llyfr Gruffudd ap Nicolas'. This manuscript was produced to a very high standard: 'In point of production, no Welsh manuscript of s.xv [the fifteenth century] aims at comparable grandeur; the parchment is of high quality (if slightly stiff), still white; the black ink is of the best; the layout is careful and generous; the script [...] is large and expert'.[85] The level of production led Daniel Huws to

---

[81] Smith, 'Fosterage, Adoption, and God-parenthood', p. 25.

[82] *LlIor*, §94/10; *LTMW*, p. 126, ll. 9–12.

[83] Jenkins, *LTMW*, p. 386, discusses the term and the etymological implication that there was a building on the land; other examples in the laws suggest the opposite, and this may simply be enclosed land.

[84] *LT*, X42, Q78, and p. 236.

suggest that this manuscript was commissioned by Gruffudd ap Nicolas of Dinefwr in Carmarthenshire, south-west Wales.[86]

It is not only the production of 'Llyfr Gruffudd ap Nicolas' which is ambitious. The text within the manuscript is as remarkable as its production, as the text has been heavily re-edited and reorganized.[87] The scribe had access to a number of exemplars, including a Blegywryd redaction text. This was his starting point, but after copying a section, the scribe added material on the same subject from his other exemplars, starting with a Iorwerth text, which he used heavily. Huws notes that he was 'giving priority to substance rather than form'.[88] The scribe also had a large collection of triads and a collection of *damweiniau*: both are shared with a Iorwerth manuscript in the hand of Lewys Glyn Cothi, siglum K (NLW, Peniarth MS 40). The Iorwerth text used in Q is very similar indeed to the text in the second half of J (Jesus College, Oxford, MS 57), a manuscript which has a full Blegywryd text followed by portions of a Iorwerth text.[89] The two scribes were probably using the same exemplar.

As Q is a Blegywryd manuscript, the short text on rearing a child included in the Law of Women in Blegywryd redaction manuscripts was copied as part of the Law of Women. However, the scribe also copied the Iorwerth text on Children and Parents in full, immediately following the Law of Women from Blegywryd. The scribe's editing process was to copy his tractate from his Blegywryd text, but to copy the Iorwerth equivalent selectively; he would only do so if the text was different to the Blegywryd one already included. This tractate on Children and Parents is not found in the Blegywryd texts and was probably a new composition for the Iorwerth redaction, and so it was copied into Q after the Blegywryd text. A similar process of selection from a Iorwerth text was at work in J, but in J there is a Blegywryd text followed by the Iorwerth material as a block, whereas in Q the Iorwerth material is interspersed and inserted throughout the manuscript after Blegywryd sections on the same subject. The Iorwerth tractate also occurs in another fifteenth-century composite Blegywryd manuscript: S (British Library (BL), Add. MS 22,356), but the text is not complete. §6 to §7.11 occurs as a block in S, and then later on in the manuscript a short passage from §4 is given in a section containing miscellaneous material, but not all of §4 is presented.[90] It may be that the exemplar the scribe of S was using was not complete.

---

[85] *RWMS*, Wynnstay 36, p. 485.

[86] *RWMS*, Wynnstay 36, p. 485.

[87] Sara Elin Roberts, 'Creu Trefn o Anhrefn: Gwaith Copïydd Testun Cyfreithiol', *National Library of Wales Journal*, 32.4 (2002), pp. 397–420; Roberts, *Growth of Law*, pp. 165–68.

[88] *RWMS*, Wynnstay 36, p. 485.

[89] Roberts, *Growth of Law*, pp. 167–68.

[90] Christine James, *Machlud Cyfraith Hywel: Golygiad Beirniadol ac Eglurhaol o Lsgr. BL Add. 22356 (S)*, Texts and Studies in Medieval Welsh Law (Seminar Cyfraith Hywel, 2013), <http://cyfraith-hywel.org.uk/cy/machlud-cyf-hyw.php>, §§1967–99, labelled 'Gwadu Mab' ('Denying a Son'), and §§2475–78, in a section labelled 'Amrywion' ('Miscellaneous').

Several *damweiniau* on the subject of children and parents are included in the large collection of *damweiniau* found in Q. The *damweiniau* collections are organized by form rather than by subject matter, although there is some structure within the collections.[91] The *damweiniau* presented in this edition are not consecutive in the text in Q. They are included as they are on the same subject as the other text; other material on the same topic is not common in other tractates.

Editorial Methodology

General observations

Cyfraith Hywel is a subject which lends itself well to the study of Middle Welsh, with its multitude of lengthy prose manuscripts dating from the mid-thirteenth century to the early fifteenth century: it offers a wealth of material. However, the lawtexts can be said to suffer from problems of accessibility to some extent, and dealing with their complex textual relationships and the numerous variant readings is not for the faint-hearted. Finding edited texts of the laws is also difficult: there are published texts of the laws, but despite the high number of extant medieval manuscripts, there are only a handful of edited texts of individual manuscripts, and many of those editions date from the mid-twentieth century.[92] Translations of those texts are even rarer, and that makes using a legal text for reading Middle Welsh very challenging indeed. Add to those problems the very complex textual history of the manuscripts, which makes selecting a representative manuscript for studying the law very problematic, and the length of the lawtexts, which may also be extremely off-putting. All this means that it is difficult to know where to begin when it comes to reading the lawtexts.

Selecting an accessible Middle Welsh text to represent the subject is equally challenging. One obvious option would be to present a complete edited manuscript with detailed notes. This means that the lawtext is presented in its own context, and the manuscript can be discussed in some detail before presenting the text. This is a standard approach for many medieval Welsh prose

---

[91] Roberts, *Growth of Law*, pp. 105–10.
[92] The only edition of a Iorwerth manuscript is *LlIor*, from 1960, which presents B, excluding the *Cynghawsedd* at the end of that manuscript. Wade-Evans edited V and W of the Cyfnerth manuscripts and presented an edited text, as Wade-Evans, *Welsh Medieval Law*. More recently, Cyfnerth is represented by the first part of Z, in Roberts, *Llawysgrif Pomffred*. Blegywryd is found in *LlBleg*, from 1952, but a more recent edition is *J(ed.)*, revised in 1990. More recent editions are the edition of S, whose first part is Blegywryd, in James, *Machlud*; and the edition of H, a non-redaction manuscript, in G. Angharad Elias, *Yr Ail Lyfr Du o'r Waun: Golygiad Beirniadol ac Eglurhaol o Lsgr. Peniarth 164 (H)*, Texts and Studies in Medieval Welsh Law, 5, 2 vols (Seminar Cyfraith Hywel, 2018).

texts. However, the complete texts tend to be extremely lengthy; even the shorter manuscripts have well over a hundred folios. Incomplete manuscripts are naturally problematic as texts can break off where leaves are lost, and several of the law manuscripts have their end wanting. In addition, selecting a complete manuscript presents its own problems: the manuscripts fit into groups of texts similar in order and content, known as redactions, but the redactions have different features; studying a text of one of the redactions excludes texts found in the others. While having a single-manuscript text where a reader can start at the beginning and proceed systematically to the end seems a logical approach, this is not always a practical option for the Welsh law manuscripts.

The alternative is to select sections of the law to study. The lawtexts are arranged, on the whole, into subject-specific sections — or, alternatively, texts organized by genre — known as tractates. Several of these tractates form stand-alone sections, and four of the tractates have been the subject of comparative editions (taking a text from the different redactions of the laws, although Blegywryd versions were not included)[93] with translations into English and including essays on various aspects of the text, made under the auspices of Seminar Cyfraith Hywel.[94] This brings us closer to presenting a complete picture of a section of law, and it is a useful way to proceed. There are some drawbacks, of course — first, it does not include all of the discussions on a particular topic, since the tractates are not exhaustive, and subjects are discussed in the laws in different contexts. For example, there is a tractate on the Value of Wild and Tame, discussing animals, but animals are also discussed under contract law, theft, compensation for injury, the Corn Damage section on damage to crops by animals, in the triads, and in the model pleadings inter alia. While the single-tractate studies by Seminar Cyfraith Hywel are excellent and complete, producing the same tractate from different redactions as a reading text means that there is considerable overlap and repetition. Selecting a section from one redaction would avoid these problems, but would also lead to the same problems encountered when selecting the text from a single manuscript.

A third approach could combine both elements by producing an anthology of sections from different parts of the manuscripts and from a wide range of manuscripts. This has been done on two occasions and in Welsh-language publications both times. The first was by Stephen J. Williams in 1938, which offers a version in Modern Welsh of various interesting sections from the manuscripts, but this is not helpful for reading Middle Welsh. The Preface notes that 'Paratowyd y llyfryn hwn yn bennaf ar gyfer pobl na allant ym-drafferthu â darllen testunau Cymraeg Canol, ond a hoffai wybod rhywbeth am gyfreithiau cynnar y Cymry' ('This booklet was prepared mainly for people who

---

[93] *WLW*, p. 132.
[94] *WLW*, *LAL*, *WKC*, *TCC*. The triads are also a tractate, and they have been edited in *LT*.

cannot go to the trouble of reading Middle Welsh texts, but who would like to know something about the early laws of the Welsh').⁹⁵ The author explains that anybody truly wishing to study the laws would need to turn to the original texts. The selection was made from two manuscripts of one redaction only, although not exclusively so, and the texts were chosen because they were the 'least complex' (*lleiaf astrus*) and because they shed light on social aspects of the 'old Welsh world' (*yr hen fyd Cymreig*) rather than 'the political and military system' (*y gyfundrefn wleidyddol a milwrol*): perhaps a poignant reflection of the time in which it was produced.⁹⁶ The second example is more recent, and lengthier. *Archwilio Cymru'r Oesoedd Canol: Testunau o Gyfraith Hywel* presents around twenty extracts from different parts of the laws, but with a text from each of the three Welsh redactions where possible.⁹⁷ This gives a fuller overview of the laws, but there is some repetition between the versions presented, although it allows for comparison of the different redactions. Creating a curated anthology in this way allows for more variety and a better overview of a range of subjects discussed in Welsh law, but any selection is likely to be subjective, and the omissions may be more telling than the inclusions.

All of these approaches were considered, and the text presented here can be seen as including elements of all three options — but that is not to say that the problems arising from selecting any of the methods have been avoided. At one point, the plan was to present an edition from a single manuscript, a Iorwerth redaction text since there is only one edition of a Iorwerth text in existence. A short Iorwerth manuscript was selected, but the reason for its brevity was because it was laconic, and so it did not have all of the law that would be expected in a Iorwerth manuscript. This was not necessarily a problem, but the tractates which had gaps due to missing pages were less than ideal. This idea was discarded when it became apparent that a large part of the surviving text was the very lengthy Iorwerth section on Land Law, and while that has its value, it is difficult in parts and somewhat long-winded. Instead, it was decided to select a tractate, but to avoid the four tractates which have already been studied (Women, Suretyship, the Law of the Court, and the Three Columns of Law). Some of the remaining tractates are very long — Land Law, the Value of Wild and Tame — and others have been studied in other places (triads, *Cyfar*). Several of the under-studied tractates deserve the detailed and more interdisciplinary treatment given to the four longer volumes. Looking to the Iorwerth redaction, which has only been edited in full once, one tractate stood out as being longer than a paragraph but less likely to be included as a book-length

---

⁹⁵ Stephen J. Williams, *Detholion o'r Hen Gyfreithiau Cymreig* (Cardiff, 1938), p. vii.
⁹⁶ Williams, *Detholion*, p. vii.
⁹⁷ Sara Elin Roberts and Christine James, *Archwilio Cymru'r Oesoedd Canol: Testunau o Gyfraith Hywel*, Texts and Studies in Medieval Welsh Law, 4 (Seminar Cyfraith Hywel, 2015).

study presenting different versions along with discussions or studies of particular aspects. This is the text labelled 'Family Law' by Dafydd Jenkins. It discusses the rights of children, coming of age, and paternity cases. This is not a text which occurs in the Blegywryd or Cyfnerth redactions in this form, and it may have been rewritten for the Iorwerth texts. However, there is a comparative element without repetition since there is a short text on the subject of rearing children found within the Law of Women in the Blegywryd texts.

Only one of the eight Iorwerth manuscripts has been edited in full, and this forms the basis of the published edition of *Llyfr Iorwerth* (*LlIor*). Of the remaining seven manuscripts, the section occurs in six of the manuscripts, but it is incomplete in two of those. It does not occur in A (NLW, Peniarth MS 29: *Llyfr Du'r Waun* ('The Black Book of Chirk')). However, the text presented here is not taken from one of the Iorwerth manuscripts, but from Q (NLW, Wynnstay MS 36), a manuscript which belongs primarily to the Blegywryd redaction, but which includes material from several other sources including Iorwerth redaction material. Children and Parents is found in Q, in full, and so it presents a later version of the material found in the earlier Iorwerth manuscripts, with Q dating from the fifteenth century but preserving an older text in this case. The Blegywryd section is also found in Q, and other sections on the same subject — taken from collections of *damweiniau* — are also present and included here, several of these edited for the first time in 180 years and only available in print in *AL* before now. The advantage of using this manuscript as the basis for the text presented here is that everything is from the same text. The Iorwerth text can be compared with the edition in *LlIor*, and other texts are included for comparison. The reader may become familiar with the (very regular) orthography and language used by the scribe, and it is an example of fifteenth-century prose writing in Middle Welsh.

Language and orthography

The text has been transcribed from the manuscript and edited, with punctuation, capitalization, and paragraphing added following modern standards. Editorial interference has been kept to a minimum, and the orthography of the scribe has been maintained throughout. In cases of eye-skip, where the scribe has omitted words or letters which are necessary for the sense, the text has been amended with the insertion of the missing words taken from other versions of the same text where possible, and these are inserted between square brackets. The insertions are all taken from Q's sister-manuscript, J. Otherwise, the manuscript's original reading has been kept as far as is possible, with any rare scribal errors amended and the original reading given at the bottom of the page using alphabetically arranged lowercase letters as the footnote mark. There are fewer than fifteen insertions and emendations in this text.

Spelling system

There has been no standardization of spelling in cases with variant forms, for example *gyssefin, gysseuyn*; *pennkenedyl, penkenedyl*. Only one form is listed in the glossary unless the variant spelling is likely to mislead, in which case a cross-reference is given. The scribe's spelling is generally consistent, with rare variations. The main aspects of the system are noted below, with the corresponding spelling in Modern Welsh (ModW).

Spelling	Sound	ModW	Notes
<c>	/k/	<c>	
<k>	/k/	<c>	As initial consonant
<k>	/k/	<c>	Four examples, in medial position in combination with <c> e.g. *dycker*.
<d>	/d/	<d>	
<d>	/ð/	<dd>	One exception: §3.9, *vaeddu*. One example of <dh> for /ð/: §3.1, *vedho*.
<f>	/v/	<f>	In medial position
<v>	/v/	<f>	In the initial position
<u>	/v/	<f>	In medial position followed by a vowel
<g>	/ŋ/	<ng>	
<g>	/g/	<g>	
<p>	/b/	<b>	Particularly at the end of words
<r>	/r/	<r>	
<r>	/rh/	<rh>	
<t>	/d/	<d>	
<u>	/ʉ/	<u>	
<v>	/ʉ/	<u>	In initial position in numeral *vn*, consistently; other words in two examples, *vchelɼr* and *vchot*.
<ɞ>	/u/	<w>	One exception: *ardelu* where <u> is used for /u/. This may betray the orthography of the source.
<y>	/ə/	<y>	Unstressed words, monosyllables.
<y>	/ɨ/	<i>	Stressed monosyllables and final syllables. Common as unstressed grammatical words e.g. possessives, particles. (See Glossary.)

Mutations

Initial mutations can be problematic in Middle Welsh (MW) texts: not only do the rules of mutation not correspond fully to modern practice, but we cannot be confident either that mutations, especially lenition, were always rendered in the orthography.[98] The tables below give examples of how the mutations are represented in the text, giving the ModW initial consonant change, and examples of the mutated forms in MW.

The soft mutation can be seen in some cases, but orthographical practices mean that in other cases it is not possible to see the mutation. However, the mutations are not consistently shown, and there are examples of words where the initial soft mutation would be expected in ModW but it is omitted in the text.

Soft mutation

c > g	*dḇy gyfelin, yn gyntaf, neu geinaḇc*
p > b	*ar ben, bieu*
	But not always shown: see *o pedeir, a perthyn*
t > d	Sometimes seen: *a'e dat, dros*
	But *a tyfo, ar tir*: failure to render in the orthography
	No examples of <t> for /d/ where there is no mutation
b > f	*o vrethyn, y vlḇydyn, yny vo*
d > dd	*a dylyir, pedeir blyned ar dec*: failure to render in the orthography
	<d> used for /ð/ and /d/
g > -	*vn ḇreic, a'e orchymyn* [g omitted]
ll > l	*y laḇ*
m > f	*y vab, y vam, y ḇreic vut*
rh > r	*nyt reit, a rodi*: failure to render in the orthography
	<r> used for /r/ and /rh/

In this text, and the same is true of many MW texts, the nasal mutation is not shown as it would be expected in ModW in this text. Forms such as the ones in the table below are found, but the presentation of the nasal mutation can be problematic due to the orthography. This is a common feature of MW texts, and the nasal mutation is only seen in later periods. The grammatical situations where initial mutations occur are not discussed here, and students should use reference works to familiarize themselves with this aspect.[99]

Nasal mutation

c > ng(h)	*y galhon, y kymḇt*: failure to render in the orthography
	Scribe uses <g> to represent /ŋ/ (<ng> in ModW)
p > mh	e.g. *ym penn*

---

[98] *GMW*, p. 17.
[99] For example, *GMW*, pp. 14-23.

t > nh   No examples in this text
b > m   e.g. *ymreint*
d > n   No examples in this text
g > ng   Failure to render in the orthography
         Scribe uses <g> to represent /ŋ/ (<ng> in ModW)

The aspirate mutation is commonly shown for all initial consonants affected.

Aspirate mutation
c > ch   *kynny chaffo, a'e chnuf*
p > ph   *a phatell, na phenkenedyl*
t > th   *y that, a thri*

'Sandhi *h*', the addition of *h-* to words starting with vowels following third singular pronouns, is also shown in this text.[100] There are two examples, both in the first section: *a'e hoen, a'e hymduc*.

These initial consonant mutations should be remembered when using the glossary; misleading forms have been listed under their mutated form with a cross-reference to help with looking up words.

Common constructions and forms

The language of the text shows many aspects which are typical of the legal texts as a whole, including sentences conveying emphasis, imperatives, and heavy use of the subjunctive: the aim of the law is to provide rules for situations which may occur, rather than to state what is happening or what has happened. Impersonal (blame free!) forms are also used in the text. There are several technical terms and usages in this text which are specific to the laws — these include the words used for different fines (*camlwrw* and *dirwy*) and the verb *dwyn*, which in this text is used to refer to the affiliation of the child, although ordinarily it would simply mean 'to bring'. Common constructions used in the laws include the conditional structure which introduces *damweiniau* sentences: *O derfydd, O deruyd, Or deruyd*, which combines the conditional conjunction *o* ('if') with the consuetudinal present third singular form with a future sense of *darfod* ('to happen'). A very common verb used in the laws is *dyly*, the third-person present of *dyly, dylÿu*, a defective verb in ModW but complete in all forms in MW. This is used for things which must be done in the laws — 'a man is to do something' — or for entitlements or something which is right for someone to have or do. The sense is stronger in Middle Welsh than perhaps it is in Modern English, as the things which are to be done (using *dyly*) are obligatory, unlike the English equivalent, 'should'. Negatives and demonstratives also feature heavily in the laws, as the purpose of the lawtexts is to tell

---

[100] See *GMW*, §26; and Patrick Sims-Williams, 'Sandhi *h* after Third-Person Pronouns in Middle Welsh', *Celtica*, 34 (2022), pp. 60–86.

people what should be done and how it is to be done, and to state what is not permitted.

Chapter numbering and presentation

The text presented here has been divided into sequentially numbered sections, starting with §1. It is the usual practice to number sections and sentences in editions of Welsh lawtexts — unlike with poetry, line numbers may change according to the format.[101] *LlIor* has section numbers, but in its own cross-references it uses section numbers and (unprinted) line numbers. (Reference to *LlIor* in this work is to section number and sentence number.) In the four tractate studies, the text presented from Iorwerth maintains the same section numbers for the equivalent section of text, and this is useful since it 'fixes' the number for the section.[102] Therefore, in those editions, the first section of text is not numbered §1: the first section of the Iorwerth text in *WLW*, for example, is §44, as that is the section number of the first part of the Law of Women in the *LlIor* edition. The Iorwerth sections edited here are §§97 to 103 in *LlIor*, but while it is useful to maintain the same section number across different editions, it is not practical in this case. The text presented here is not all from Iorwerth: this edition opens with a section from Blegywryd, and ends with a selection of *damweiniau*. Therefore, the sections here have been numbered sequentially, starting at §1 and ending at §9.

There are no chapter headings in this text, and neither is the tractate labelled, partly because the first section is from Blegywryd and the last is a collection of *damweiniau*. Jenkins called the tractate 'Family Law', and Wiliam labelled it 'Children' in his conspectus.[103] Owen only gave a few words' description to different sections, e.g. 'Of the foetus of a woman, if injured', in his table of contents, and his text makes it clear that these are a translation of the headings found (only) in manuscript C (BL, Cotton MS Caligula A III), which is a thirteenth-century manuscript.[104] There are otherwise no titles in the manuscripts themselves and no introduction to the section in any of the manuscripts. The titles in C are useful, but C is missing the latter part of the section and so there are only four surviving titles, and the second part of the text would be very long.

---

[101] Recent editions have done this: James, *Machlud*; Elias, *Yr Ail Lyfr Du*; Roberts, *Llawysgrif Pomffred*. AL has books, chapters, and numbered sentences, but neither Wade-Evans's *Welsh Medieval Law* nor *LlBleg* has this, although *LlBleg* added chapter headings, and the same headings were used in J(ed.), with more added, as the second half of J is not found in *LlBleg*.

[102] 'The reference system is that of Wiliam's *Llyfr Iorwerth*, with the addition of numbers for the sentences of that edition: thus §44/10 is the tenth sentence of §44 there.' *WLW*, p. 161.

[103] *LTMW*, p. 129; *LlIor*, p. xliv.

[104] *AL*, table of contents; *AL*, VC II.xxviii–xxxi.

The text here has been divided into several sections, starting with the Blegywryd text, and with the *damweiniau* given one section number as they are a genre and from a collection of *damweiniau*. The Iorwerth text is the longest, and it is divided into seven sections. Aneurin Owen divided the same text in *AL* into four chapters in VC II, xxviii–xxxi, taking as his guide the titles in manuscript C. In *LlIor*, Aled Rhys Wiliam organized the text into sections, numbered §§97–103, and the present edition follows the same text divisions. The second part of the text, from *LlIor*, §100 to the end, does not have as many obvious divisions, but Wiliam's divisions are sensible and thematic. The Iorwerth text follows the same order in all of the manuscripts.

The manuscript is bicolumnar throughout, and is foliated; the modern foliation is used here rather than the older (defective) seventeenth-century foliation. Emendations to the text have been noted in square brackets. Where the text has been corrected, the original form in the manuscript is given as a footnote, using lowercase letters of the alphabet.

The text presented here is found as follows in Q, NLW Wynnstay MS 36:

§1	fols 80vb–81ra
§§2–8	fols 84rb–87ra
§9.1–3	fol. 87rb
§9.4–5	fols 106rb–106va
§9.6–15	fols 109vb–110rb
§9.16–17	fol. 112vb

TEXT

§1

¹G6reic a geiff y gan dat y mab yr y vagu [kyhyt ac y dy6etp6yt vry], peis[a] a talo pedeir keina6c, a buch de6isseit, a phatell a talo keinha6c a dimei, a charreit o'r yt goreu a tyfo ar tir y tat, a hynny a perthyn y tayogeu.

²Mab bonhedic a dylyir y vagu val hyn: mam y mab[b] gyssefin a'e hymduc na6 mis yn y chroth. ³A thri mis g6edy y ganher, hi a'e mac, a hynny yn lle bl6ydyn idi. ⁴Odyna y tat a dyly keissa6 ida6 y holl gyfreideu: yn gyntaf y dyry dauat a'e chnuf ac a'e hoen genti. ⁵Ac odyna g6eren neu geina6c, a phadell hayarn neu pedeir keina6c kyfreith, a muneit o 6enith y 6neuthur i6t ida6; a charreit deu ychen o gynnut, a d6y gyfelin o vrethyn g6yn neu vn brith ar y mab. ⁶A buch vlith a'e llo, a thri charreit o 6enith a heid a cheirch, a thri charreit o gynnut. ⁷Os myn y vam, hi a'e kciff oll; onys myn, rothcr y arall.

§2

¹Rei yssyd yn pedrussa6 am veichogi g6reic, peth a dylyir amdana6, ae 6yneb6erth ae galanas. ²Kyfreith a dy6eit pan y6 galanas a dylyir amdana6. ³Sef achos y6 hynny, yn y tri mis kyntaf y byd g6yn ef, ac y byd trayan galanas arna6; yn y tri mis perued y byd rud, ac y byd deuparth galanas arna6; yn y tri mis di6ethaf y byd kyfla6n o aelodeu ac eneit, ac y byd galanas c6byl arna6.

⁴Rei a dy6eit nat ia6nach talu galanas g6r ymdana6 noc vn 6reic, cany 6ys peth y6, ae g6r ae g6reic. ⁵Kyfreith a dy6eit bot yn ia6naf galanas g6r arna6, kanys [ia6naf] y6 barnu yn ol y peth pennaf, a hynny yny vedydyer. ⁶Canys pob dyn a holer a dylyir y holi yn her6yd y en6,[c] ac ny 6ybydir yny vedydyer, ac 6rth hynny y byd ar vreint[d] y beichogi.

⁷Ac 6rth hynny y dylyant talu drosta6 a thygu hyt pan el yn y seith ml6yd, eithyr na dylyant talu na dir6y na chaml6r6 y'r brenhin drosta6. ⁸Cany dyly y brenhin am annodeu dim, nac am 6eithret dyn ynvyt, ac nat oes b6yll gantha6 ynteu. ⁹Ef a dyly hagen dieissya6 y colledic o'r eida6.

¹⁰O benn y seithvet mlyned allan, ef ehun bieu tygu drosta6 a'e tat bieu talu, canys yna y dyt ef y mab a dan la6 y perigla6r, ac y byd arna6 g6ed Du6.

---

[a] hanner peis Q
[b] ma Q
[c] yn6 Q
[d] veint Q

§3

¹O'r pan aner^a y mab yny vo pedeir bl6yd ar dec y dyly vot 6rth noe y tat, a'e dat yn argl6yd arna6, ac ny dyly vot arna6 cosp neb namyn h6nn y tat, namyn ar vn geina6c namyn a vedho y tat. ²Ac ny dyly vot mar6ty arna6 yn gyhyt a hynny o amser, namyn bot yn eida6 y tat y holl da, canys yn hynny o amser y dyly atteb drosta6 o pob peth.

³O'r byd mar6 y tat y vl6ydyn gyntaf y ganer y mab, ef ehun yna a a ymreint y dat. ⁴Ny dylyir talu ebedi6 mab yny vo pedeir bl6yd ar dec a'e tat yn vy6. ⁵G6edy del ef ymreint y tat, ehun a'e tal.

⁶Ym pen y pedeir blyned ar dec y dyly y tat d6yn y vab at yr argl6yd a'e orchymyn ida6. ⁷Ac yna y mae ia6n ida6 g6rhav y'r argl6yd, a bot 6rth vreint yr argl6yd. ⁸Ac ehun a dyly vot drosta6 am pob peth ar a holer ida6. ⁹Ac ny dyly tat y vaeddu m6y noc estra6n o hynny allan. ¹⁰Ac os maed gan g6yna6 ohona6, ef a 6na ia6n ida6 o'e sarhaet, ac a vyd dir6yus.

¹¹O'r byd mar6 y mab o pedeir bl6yd ar dec allan ac na bo etiued ida6, yr argl6yd a dyly y da yn g6byl, ac a dyly vot yn lle mab ida6, a mar6ty vyd y ty. ¹²Ac o'r oet h6nn6 allan y byd vn vreint a bonhedic kanh6ynna6l, canyt oes vreint ida6 namyn y voned, ac nat a^b ynteu ymreint y tat yny vo mar6 y tat, ac na byd marcha6c neb yny ysgynno.

§4

¹Merch 6edy bedydyer yny seith mlyned hyt pan vo, ny dyly mynet yn ll6. ²O'r pan aner^c yny vo deudec ml6yd y dyly vot 6rth noe y that. ³O hynny allan y da6 bronneu a chedor arnei, ac y blodeua, ac yna y byd oet idi y rodi y 6r; hi a dyly vedu yr eidi. ⁴Kynny chaffo hi y rodi y 6r, hi a dyly vedu yr eidi, ac ny byd 6rth noe y that onyt hi ehunan a'e mynn; ac ny dyly y tat talu amobyr dros y verch onyt ehun a'e mynn, o'e vot yn rodyat arnei. ⁵Os ynteu ehun a'e ryd hi, kymeret veicheu y gan y neb a'e kymero.

⁶O'r deudec mlyned allan hyt ym penn y pedeir blyned ar dec y dyly vot heb veichogi, ac odyna hyt ym penn y deugeint mlyned y dyly hi ymd6yn; ac o hynny allan nyt a galanas arnei, na ll6 heuyt pryt na bo plant idi, canys diheu vyd yna na byd plant idi.

§5

¹P6y bynnac a vynno g6adu mab yn gyfreitha6l, nyt reit ida6 y 6adu yny dycker yn gyfreitha6l gysseuyn; canyt reit y neb atteb yn annolo, canys anolo y6 pob peth ny bo kyfreitha6l. ²Pa 6reic bynnac a vynno [d6yn] mab yn gyfreitha6l, val

---

^a a aner Q
^b a a Q
^c a aner Q

hynn y mae idi y dƀyn. ³Dyuot hi a'r mab hyt yr eglƀys y bo y ƀydua yndi, a dyuot hyt ar yr allaƀr, a dodi y llaƀ deheu ar yr allaƀr a'r creireu a'r llaƀ asseu ar ben y mab, ac velly tygu y Duƀ yn y blaen ac y'r allaƀr honno ac y'r creireu da yssyd arnei ac y vedyd y mab "na ry greus tat y galhon mam y mab hƀnnƀ[a] namyn y gƀr a'r gƀr (erbyn y enƀ) y'm calhon i". ⁴Ac velly y dylyir dƀyn mab y Gymro.

⁵Ac val hyn y dylyir dƀyn mab y alltut. ⁶Dyuot hyt yr eglƀys y kymero ef y dyfƀr sƀyn a'e vara offeren yndi, ac yna y dƀyn idaƀ ynteu megys y dyƀespƀyt vchot. ⁷Ac yna iaƀn y'r tat gƀneuthur vn o deu peth, ae kymryt y mab yn gyfreithaƀl ae ƀadu yn gyfreithaƀl. ⁸Os y ƀadu a vynn, iaƀn idaƀ dyuot hyt yr eglƀys a dyƀedassam ni vchot, a rodi y laƀ deheu ar yr allaƀr a'r creireu a vo arnei,[b] a'r llaƀ asseu ar ben y mab, ac velly tygu y Duƀ yn y blaen ac y'r allaƀr honno ac y'r creireu da yssyd arnei ac y'r gƀr a'e gƀahanƀys ef o gredigaeth tat a mam, na re greus ef y mab hƀnnƀ y galon y ƀreic honno erioet ac nat oes dauyn o'e ƀaet yndaƀ onyt o Adaf. ⁹O deruyd idaƀ ynteu keissiaƀ oet am y lƀ, ef a dyly oet hyt trannoeth. ¹⁰O deruyd idi hitheu keissiaƀ oet y geissiaƀ creireu, ny dyly oet namyn tridieu, cany dyly hi geisiaƀ creireu namyn y kymƀt ehun.

§6

¹O deruyd y dat gƀadu mab o genedyl gƀedy dyccer idaƀ, ny eill hƀnnƀ kaffel tat vyth gƀedy. ²Sef achaƀs yƀ hynny, y vam a'e dƀc ef yn gyfreithaƀl y tat a'e gƀadƀys, ac ƀrth hynny ny eill hitheu y dƀyn ef y dat arall eilƀeith vyth. ³Y tat a'e gƀadƀys ynteu yn gyfreithaƀl, ny byd cardychƀel ynteu byth ar hƀnnƀ dracheuyn, kanyt adƀna kyfreith a ƀnel. ⁴Y mab hƀnnƀ ƀeithion ƀrth genedyl y vam y byd y vreint, ac o llad ef dyn, kenedyl y vam a dal deuparth yr alanas, a'r trayan arnaƀ ynteu y llofrud. ⁵Ac o lledir ynteu, kenedyl y vam a dyly deuparth y alanas, a hƀnnƀ yƀ vn o dri dygyngoll kenedyl.

⁶Arall yƀ bei darffei y ƀr lad arall a meichiaƀ o genedyl y llofrud ar yr alanas, a chyn talu yr alanas dƀyn o'e vam y llofrud y dat arall, y gyfreith a dyƀeit pan yƀ y genedyl a veichiƀs ar yr alanas bieu y thalu o deu achaƀs: o ƀneuthur y gyflauan tra vu ar eu breint ƀy, ac o dylyu talu o'r neb a veichƀys.

⁷Trydyd[c] yƀ, o rodir Kymraes y alltut a bot mab idi o'r alltut, a llad dyn ohonaƀ, deuparth yr alanas a daƀ ar genedyl y vam, a'r trayan ar y llofrud; a hynny ƀrth nad oes genedyl tat a'e talo. ⁸A hƀnnƀ a elƀir yn ƀarthec deuach, ƀrth vot yn dir diueichieu ar y gƀarthec hynny, canys a gƀarthec y telit pop tal gynt.

⁹Y deu uab a dyƀedassam ni vchot, vn vreint ac vn ƀerth ac vn sarhaet ynt a bonhedic kanhƀynaƀl.

---

[a] eye-skip in J
[b] arei Q
[c] Tryd Q

§7

¹Mab deolef a vyd, a mab diodef. ²Sef y6 mab deolef, mab a dy6etto y 6reic ar y thauot leueryd, ac nys dycco y'r dygyn; h6nn6 a ellir y 6adu pan vynner. ³Mab diodef y6 mab a dycco g6reic yn gyfreitha6l, a diodef vn dyd a bl6ydyn; ny ellir y 6adu o hynny allan vyth. ⁴Or deruyd y h6nn6 6neuthur kyflauan, ny ellir y 6adu yn yr yg, kanny 6ad6yt yn yr ehag 6rth y vot yn vap diodef.

⁵Kyt boet y brenhin a vo tat y vab alltudes, a g6adu ohona6, alltut vyd y vab o hynny allan. ⁶Os alltut a 6atta mab Kymraes, bonhedic canh6yna6l vyd h6nn6 o hynny allan, canys 6rth vreint y vam y byd pob mab g6edy g6atter.

⁷Tat a diga6n trannoeth 6adu y mab g6edy di6ycko y gyfulauan drosta6, os myn.

⁸O deruyd y tat rodi da yr meithrin mab, ny dyly 6edy hynny y 6adu, canys trydyd kymeryat y6 ar vab.

⁹Or deruyd mar6 y tat, y pennkenedyl a eill y 6adu ar y seithvet, vn 6ed ac y g6attei y tat bei by6, ac yn yr vn egl6ys, a seith ganta6 o oreug6yr kenedyl gan y ll6 6ynt vot yn lan y l6 ef. ¹⁰Ony byd pennkenedyl, vn g6r ar hugeint o oreug6yr a'e g6ata.

¹¹Her6yd g6yr Po6ys, ony byd na that na phenkenedyl, dec 6yr a deugeint a'e kymer ac a'e g6atta.

¹²Ny diga6n neb yᵃ dyg6ydo tir y mab yn y la6 y 6adu yr y yrruᵇ ohona6; ny eill bra6t 6adu y gilyd, ac ony byd bra6t, ny eill keuender6 y 6adu yr y yrru ohona6. ¹³Ac o deruyd bot rei o genedyl mab yn y 6adu, ac ereill yn y gymryt gan y ll6 nac yr gobyr nac er g6erth y maent yn y gymryt, ia6nnaf y6 credu yr rei yssyd yn y gymryt, canys gnotaafᶜ y6 [g6adu] y mab yr tref y tat.

¹⁴Pob bra6t a diga6n g6adu y ch6aer, onyt yn vn lle: rac rannu da y mam a'e that a hi, ny ellir. ¹⁵Ac velly pop alltut a diga6n g6adu y vra6t neu y ch6aer os mynn, onyt rac kyfuranu o da eu mam a'e tat ac 6ynt, neu rac di6c eu kyfulauan a 6nel6ynt.

§8

¹Val hynn y dylyir kymryt mab y genedyl: y tat ehunᵈ a diga6n kymryt y mab g6edy as dycco y vam yn gyfreitha6l gysseuyn. ²Ony byd tat, penkenedyl ar y seithuet a eill y gymryt; ac sef val y kymer: kymryt o'r penkenedyl d6yla6 y mab r6g y d6yla6 ynteu, a rodi cussan ida6, canys ar6yd kenedyl y6 cussan. ³A g6edy hynny y rodi o'r penkenedyl y mab yn lla6 yr hynaf o'r g6yr, a rodi o h6nn6 gussan ida6, ac velly o la6 y la6 hyt at y g6r di6ethaf. ⁴Ony byd penkenedyl, vn g6r ar hugeint o oreug6yr y genedyl a'e kymer, a chymryt y mab o'r g6r a vo yn

---

ᵃ or y Q
ᵇ yrr Q
ᶜ gnottaa Q
ᵈ eu hun Q

lle yr argl6yd erbyn y la6 deheu ida6, a'e rodi yn lla6 yr hynaf o'r g6yr hynny, a rodi o h6nn6 gussan ida6; a'e gymryt o h6nn6 erbyn y lla6 deheu ida6 a'e rodi yn lla6 yr eil g6r nessaf ida6, ac velly o la6 y la6 hyt at y g6r di6ethaf o hynny o 6yr.

§9

[1] O deruyd geni dyn ac aelodeu g6r ac vn g6reic ida6, ac yn petrus py ardelu a vo ganta6, ae g6r ae g6reic; rei a dy6eit dylyu etrych o pa aruer yd aruero, ae[a] o vn g6r ae vn g6reic, a her6yd yd aruero kerdet y vreint. [2] Os o pob vn yd aruerha ef, kyfreith a dy6eit dylyu kerdet y vreint 6rth y breint ychaf; sef y6 h6nn6, breint g6r a dylyu tref tat ohona6. [3] Ac o beichogir ef, caffel o'e vab tref y tat o vreint y g6r a'e beichoges; ac or beichocca ynteu 6reic arall, caffel o'e vab ef tref y tat.

[4] Or deruyd y vab vchel6r rodi y vab ar veithrin at daya6c o ganyat y argl6yd, a'e uagu o'r taya6c vl6ydyn ae d6y ae teir, pan vo mar6 y taya6c, ony byd plant ida6, y dylyet oll a dyg6ydd yn lla6 y mab maeth. [5] Or byd plant ida6, kymeint a phop vn o'e ueibon a geiff y mab maeth.

[6] Or deruyd geni deu uab yn vn torll6yth, a'r torll6yth yn ieuaf o blant y tat, ia6n y6 y'r vam g6ybot p6y di6ethaf a anet ohonunt, 6rth gaffel y tydyn kyfreitha6l ohona6. [7] Ac yna y byd geir geir y mam y rydunt. [8] Or deruyd na 6ypper p6y di6ethaf p6y gyntaf, diheu y6 bot y neill o'r torll6yth h6nn6 yn ol, ac 6rth hynny y dylyant 6ynteu y tydyn kyfreitha6l, a h6nn6 a renir yn deu hanner y rydunt, canys kyhyded y6 y rydunt. [9] Ereill o'r ygneit a dy6eit yny 6yppo yn diheu y vot ef yn vab ieuaf, na dyly ef breint y mab ieuaf.

[10] Or deruyd g6adu merch o genedyl, a'e rodi y 6r, a bot amrysson am y hamobyr, kyfreith a dy6eit pan y6 yr argl6yd a'e dyly, canyt oes perchenna6c a'e dylyo, a h6nn6 yn diffeith brenhin y byd. [11] Os Kymraes vyd y mam, kymeint vyd y hamobyr ac vn bonhedic kanh6yna6l, nyt amgen, pedeir ar hugeint. [12] Os alltudes vyd y mam, kymeint vyd a'e mam ac vn merch alltut, nyt amgen, pedeir ar hugeint. [13] Ac velly vyd ebedi6 mab a 6atter, ony byd kynydu ohona6 o vreint mal y dyrchauo ar y ebedi6.

[14] Or deruyd tebygu bot yn uab diodef pop mab diodef a dy6etter y uot yn vab dyn, y gyfreith a dy6eit nat[b] mab diodef. [15] Sef y6 mab diodef, mab a dycco y uam yn gyfreitha6l kyny chymerer, ny 6at6yt, ac 6rth na 6ad6yt, diodeuedic y6, a h6nn6 ny ellir y 6adu rac y gyfulauan.

[16] O deruyd bot mab y 6reic vut, a'e ammeu o genedyl y tat, nyt reit y genedyl y tat na'e 6adu na'e gymryt, onys mynnant, kany dy6eit ehun y dyuot yn eidunt 6y. [17] G6edy bo mar6, ef a diga6n ymyrru ar y genedl, ony 6edir yn gyfreitha6l a'e uot yn gymeredic.

---

[a] ao Q
[b] hyt nat Q

NOTES

Cross references within the notes are to section numbers, §, and sentence numbers. See the list of grammatical abbreviations on p. xiii.

§1

1.1 **Gwreic** 'a woman'. Here *gwraig* is used, as the woman is not a virgin, *morwyn*: in the laws, there is a distinction between a *morwyn*, a 'maiden' or literally a virgin, and a mature woman, *gwraig*. *Gwraig* can also refer to a married woman, or 'wife', and it is used in this sense in ModW as well (*WLW*, p. 5; Sara Elin Roberts, '"Gwreic wyf fi": Transition to Womanhood in Medieval Wales', in *Middle-Aged Women in the Middle Ages*, ed. by Sue Niebrzydowski (D. S. Brewer, 2011), pp. 25–36 (pp. 26–29)). The text here is unspecific — she is not necessarily the wife of the man who is the father of the son (and indeed, she probably is not married to the father), and she may not even be the mother of the child.
a geiff y gan dat y mab 'receives from the father of the son'. The father pays for the son's upbringing, something which is also found in Irish law: in one Irish lawtext it is stated, *In coimpert dodentar, is a altrum ⁊ a cin forin fer*, 'The offspring who will be produced, the man is responsible for its raising and its liability' until the child is a month old, after which the kindred would be responsible (Charlene Eska, *Cáin Lánamna: An Old Irish Tract on Marriage and Divorce Law* (Brill, 2010), p. 279, §36, First Commentary to B).
yr y vagu 'for his rearing'. The items listed are *yr y vagu*, using the prep. *yr* 'for', or 'in order to' with the 3 sing. m. poss. pron. *y* referring to the son. In the Latin version of this text in Latin D, the text states *mater habebit de patre pro educacione*, 'the mother receives from the father for his education', something which is not stated elsewhere in the Welsh laws, but which is found in the Irish laws: fosterage could serve 'as a means of educating children in the skills necessary for the rank of society of which they were a member' (Eska, *Cáin Lánamna*, p. 9).

Given that this text discusses villeins specifically (the lower classes of society, bondsmen tied to the land or peasants), the Latin version may have the vestiges of rules on fosterage between families of different social classes — see also the discussion on §9.4–5, below, where a noble son is fostered by a bondsman. There were various reasons for fosterage in early medieval Ireland and Wales, but one aspect was a political act of clientship with benefits for both sides: 'The delegation of children to subordinates would be accompanied by the grant of a fief (*rath*), normally accounted in cattle, awarded by lords in exchange for allegiance from their clients' (Peter Parkes, 'Celtic Fosterage: Adoptive Kinship and Clientage in Northwest Europe', *Comparative Studies in Society and History*, 48.2 (2006), pp. 359–95 (p. 363)). Although the recognizable terminology for fosterage is not present in the Latin text or in the Welsh versions, where it is simply described as *magu*, 'rearing', this may be a description of fosterage of a noble son with a villein. The payments come from the father, to a *gwraig*, a woman, or a wife: it would be unusual for a husband to pay his wife for rearing their son, so this too seems to imply fosterage, which could start with breastfeeding.

In Math uab Mathonwy, the Fourth branch of the Mabinogi, arrangements are made by Gwydion for *meithrin* Lleu (see Ian Hughes, *Math uab Mathonwy: The Fourth Branch of the Mabinogi* (Dublin Institute for Advanced Studies, 2013), p. 10, l. 260, *ymobryn a wnaeth a'r wreic ueithryn y mab*, 'he made an agreement with the woman for rearing the child'). In her study of the text, Eleanor Smith notes that '*meithryn* means not only fosterage in the abstract but specifically breastfeeding' in this text (Eleanor Smith, 'Baptism, Kinship, and Incest in *Math uab Mathonwy*', *CMCS*, 88 (2024), pp. 1–19 (p. 5)).

On rearing babies in medieval England, see Nicholas Orme, *Medieval Children* (Yale University Press, 2001), pp. 56–64.

kyhyt ac y dyѵetpѵyt vry 'as much as was stated above'. There is a case of eye-skip in Q here, and instead of these words — taken from J, although they occur in all of the other Blegywryd versions of the text — Q has *a hanner peis*, 'and half a tunic', which does not make sense, see below, §1.1, *peis*. The words here prove that this text was copied from a written source, but it is uncertain to what the text is referring: if the reference is to a previous part of the Law of Women, there is nothing obvious stating clearly what would be paid to the mother of the son. It may be a reference to a comment on *ysgar*, 'separation', when a woman is pregnant (*J(ed.)*, p. 61, ll. 27–30), although in the Blegywryd text there is no detail on the items which are to be provided. However, in the Iorwerth Law of Women there is a section on *ysgar* and rearing children, which lists items similar to those found here:

> O deruyd y ѵr ysgar a'e ѵreic a hi yn ueichaѵc pan ysgarer a hi, gatter idi o'r pan ysgarher a hi yny angho yg kyueir hanher blѵydyn o ueithrin y mab. Ac gwedy ganher y mab hitheu bieu y ueithrin ef eilweith ulѵydyn — mynho na uynho ys dir idi y ueithrin yr da y gan y gѵr. Sef yѵ messur y da: buѵch ulith, a pheis a talo pedeir keinyaѵc kyureith, a phadell a talo i keinyaѵc a charreit o'r yt goreu a tyuo ar tref y dat, a hynny idi yr y ueithrin ulѵydyn. Hitheu ehun gѵedy hynny bieu y

ueithrin ef hanner blǒydyn. Ac o hynny allan ny ellir kymell erni y ueithrin namyn y rann ehun, onys mynn ehun.

If it happens that a man parts with his wife and she is pregnant when he parts from her, the period from the parting until she gives birth is to be allowed her as six months' rearing the child. And after the child is born it is for her to rear him for a further year — whether she be willing or not, she must rear him in exchange for goods from the man. This is the measure of the goods: a milch cow and a tunic worth four legal pence and a dish worth one penny and a car-load of the best corn that may grow on the holding of his father, and that goes to her for rearing him for a year. After that she herself is to rear him for six months. And from then on she cannot be compelled to rear him except for her own share, unless she herself wishes it. (*WLW*, Iorwerth §49.2–3)

peis a talo pedeir keinaǒc 'a tunic which is worth four pence'. Q actually reads *a hanner peis*, 'and half a tunic', which does not make any sense; this may have been affected by the eye-skip in the sentence where *kyhyt ac y dyǒetpǒyt vry* has been omitted. *A talo* (modern orthography *a dalo*), literally 'which pays', but with the wider sense of 'is worth', is commonly used in the laws for listing values, e.g. in the list of the value of equipment. While *pais* often means 'petticoat' or 'underskirt', and this is the meaning in ModW, in this context it has the earlier meaning of a 'tunic' or a 'coat' (*GPC*, 'pais'). The breastfeeding woman might need different clothes allowing access, or this may be provision for better clothing befitting her status caring for a noble son. The tunic in the Iorwerth text, quoted above on §1.1, is of the same value. *Ceiniog*, 'a penny', is the coin that is referred to in the laws, but there are two types: *ceiniog cyfraith*, 'legal penny', which is the full value; and *ceiniog gwta*, 'curt penny', which would have been clipped and so was lighter in weight and had less value as a result (*LTMW*, p. 325). See also below, §1.5.

a buch deǒisseit 'and a choice cow', or 'a chosen cow', *dewisaid* as an adj. from *dewis*, 'to choose'. The form *buch* for *buwch*, 'cow', is commonly used in the laws but *buwch* is also found. The items in this first section are not explained, but a cow was valuable and could also provide milk. The Iorwerth text specifies that this is a *buwch flith*, 'a milch cow'.

a phatell a talo keinhaǒc a dimei 'and a dish which is worth a penny and a halfpenny', *patell*, or *padell* in modern orthography, from the Latin *patella*, meaning 'a pan, a dish, a bowl'. In the Iorwerth text, the dish is only worth one legal penny, and it would presumably be used for feeding or even bathing the baby. Jenkins notes that the *dimai* was a third of the legal penny, and 1½ curt pence made a legal penny (*LTMW*, p. 325).

a charreit o'r yt goreu a tyfo ar tir y tat 'and a car-load of the best corn that grows on the father's land', *tyfo* in the 3 sing. pres. subj., so the best corn that it is possible to grow there. The first element of *carraid* is *car*, and the word means 'car-load'; the 'car' would be a vehicle of some sort, probably a dragged sledge originally but later with wheels (see also *GPC*, 'carraid'). This is a large amount of grain and would perhaps be for food for the mother: if she was breastfeeding, she would need to eat well. *Yd*, 'corn', was often used for crops in general, e.g. in the 'Corn Damage' section of the lawtexts (*LTMW*, p. 305).

a hynny a perthyn y tayogeu 'and that belongs to villeins', i.e. these rules are applied to the villeins (peasants, the lower classes), with *perthyn* taking the wider meaning of 'belong to' or 'pertain to'. *Tayogeu*, the pl. of *taeog*, is one of several words used for villein or bondsman: *bilain* and *aillt* are also used, the former from English 'villein' (*WLW*, pp. 217, 192, 188). The equivalent rules for higher status male children are listed next.

1.2 **Mab bonhedic** 'a nobleman, a noble son'. *Mab* may mean a son, but can also mean 'male' or 'man' (*GPC*, 'mab': 'boy, son [...] man, male'). It is not made clear whether this *mab bonheddig* is the same as a *bonheddig canhwynol*, see the note on §3.12, but *bonheddig* on its own is not a status in the laws. In the Latin versions of this section, the son is *clam adquiritur*, 'secretly conceived', which makes much more sense: it is likely that the couple are separated, or are not in a formally acknowledged marriage (see Sara Elin Roberts, 'Bells, Bulls, and Bushes: Secret Sex in the Laws', in *Cyfarwydd Mewn Cyfraith: Studies in Honour of Morfydd E. Owen*, ed. by Sara Elin Roberts, Simon Rodway, and Alexander Falileyev, Welsh Legal History Society, 17 (Welsh Legal History Society, 2022), pp. 112–123 (pp. 114–15)). In a normal situation within a family, the mother would not need specific payments from her husband, but a *mab llwyn a pherth*, the son of a secret union, would need to be reared. Giving goods for rearing a child was also an admission of paternity. In her discussion on fosterage in medieval Wales, Anderson notes that 'in the case of illegitimate princely children conceived extramaritally, fosterage effectively removed from court certain sons who might be viewed as a threat to patrimony and succession by their legitimate brothers': the situation outlined here could be a combination of both aspects, an illegitimate child and a strategic fosterage (Katharine Anderson, '*Urth Noe e Tat*: The Question of Fosterage in High Medieval Wales', *North American Journal of Welsh Studies*, 4.1 (2004), pp. 1–11 (p. 10)).

a dylyir y vagu val hyn 'is to be reared in this way'. On *magu*, 'rear, bring up, nurture, nourish', see *GPC*, 'magaf: magu'. The text is mainly focused on feeding a baby for the first year (or first eighteen months) of his life, including a discussion on breastfeeding and wet-nursing, 'the mechanical, even the mercenary, act of suckling' (Llinos Beverley Smith, 'Fosterage, Adoption and God-parenthood: Ritual and Fictive Kinship in

Medieval Wales', *Welsh History Review*, 16.1 (1992), pp. 1–35 (p. 5)). The statement that the woman receives the payments *gan dat y mab*, 'from the father of the son', shows what Smith calls 'the essential masculinity' of the transaction to arrange the suckling of the child (Smith, 'Fosterage, Adoption and God-parenthood', p. 11).

In Math, Gwydion makes the arrangements for *meithrin* Lleu, his sister's son, and it is stated that he takes the newborn baby *y rwng y dwylaw ac a gyrchwys y dref ac ef, lle y gwydat bot gwreic a bronneu genti*, 'in his two hands and went to the town with him, where he knew there was a lactating woman', lit. 'a woman with breasts' (Hughes, *Math uab Mathonwy*, p. 10, ll. 258–59). In his note on the text Hughes states that this is 'a woman with breasts [full of milk], i.e. a wet-nurse', and that this situation accords with the social convention of women other than the birth-mother breastfeeding the newborn baby (Hughes, *Math uab Mathonwy*, p. 73).

Dylyir is a form of the verb *dylyaf, dylu*, which is used throughout the laws to express either a right to something or an entitlement, or something which ought to be done (*GMW*, §165). *Dylyir* is the imps. pres./fut. ind. form, and here it conveys what compensation is to be paid for the foetus (*beichiogi*, 'pregnancy', below §2.1). Dafydd Jenkins notes that 'it is sometimes impossible to choose between the two senses, which may of course co-exist' (*LTMW*, p. 340), and states that in his translation '"it is right" is used whenever possible'. In the opening part of the Iorwerth section on Children and Parents (here §2) the sense is clearly the entitlement, the compensation for the foetus, but the other sense is also found: for example, in the opening sentence of the section on sons, it is stated: *Or pan aner y mab yny vo pedeir blwyd ar dec **y dyly vot** wrth noe y tad*, 'From when the son is born until he is fourteen years old **he is to be** by his father's dish' (Dafydd Jenkins has 'it is right for him to be'). While this could also be the son's entitlement, something which he was allowed to do, there is more of a sense of it being an obligation. The vb is complete in its forms in MW (*GMW*, §165), but in ModW it is defective, only used in the impf. and plupf., meaning 'ought to [have]', 'should [have]'.

mam y mab gyssefin 'the son's mother first', or 'first, the son's mother'. On *cysefin*, 'first', see also §5.1.

a'e hymduc 'carries him', the pron. *'e* is the 3 sing. inf. pron. with the sandhi *h* added to *ymduc* following the pronoun; it is the same form in all the texts (on this, see Patrick Sims-Williams, 'Sandhi *h* after Third-Person Pronouns in Middle Welsh', *Celtica*, 34 (2022), pp. 60–86). *Ymduc* is the 3 sing. pres. ind. of the reflexive vb *ymddwyn* (*ym* + *dwyn*), here meaning 'carry, bear' (*GPC*, 'ymddygaf' a), although it can also mean 'conceive'. See also §3.6, *ymdwyn*.

naѵ mis yn y chroth 'nine months in her womb'. The first stage of rearing the child happens before he is born, in his mother's womb, *croth*.

1.3   **A thri mis gѵedy y ganher** 'and three months after he is born', *ganher* is the imps. pres. subj. of *geni*, 'to be born', and the *y* is the obj. pron. (*gwedy* can be used without the subordinating part., *GMW*, §266).

hi a'e mac 'she rears him', *mag* from *magu*, see above §1.2; *magu* may also mean 'nourish' or 'nurse', which may mean that the mother is breastfeeding the baby. There is a focus on providing the child's needs in this text. The pron. refers to the son, not to the mother.

a hynny yn lle blѵydyn idi 'and that takes the place of a year for her', *yn lle* 'in the place, in place of': in his translation Melville Richards has 'and that is to be reckoned for a year to her' (Melville Richards, *The Laws of Hywel Dda* (Liverpool University Press, 1954), p. 68, l. 31). In other words, she spends a year rearing the child while he is in her womb for nine months, and then the first three months of his life make it a year.

When Gwydion arranges the rearing of Lleu, his sister's son, in Math, the arrangement lasts for a year: *Y mab a uagwyt y ulwydyn honno*, 'The son was reared that year' (Hughes, *Math uab Mathonwy*, p. 10, ll. 260–61). Smith argues in her study that in Math, *meithrin* is equated to breastfeeding, but it may be a combination of breastfeeding and rearing, as in this section of the laws (Smith, 'Baptism, Kinship, and Incest', p. 5).

A little earlier in the same Law of Women text, there is a note on what happens if a couple are to separate but the wife is pregnant: she is to rear the child for a year and a half.

> Ot ysgar gwr a'e wreic [gyfreithawl] a hi yn veichawc, o'r dyd yd yscarhont, kyfrifer idi y hamser y uagu yr etiued a vo yndi yna, kanys [herwyd] kyfreith blwydyn a hanner y mac y vam ef, a gwedy hynny nys mac dim.
>
> If a husband and his lawful wife are to separate when she is pregnant, from the day that they separate, let her time be calculated that she has spent rearing the heir that is in her then, because according to law his mother rears him for a year and a half, and after that she does not rear him. (*J(ed.)*, p. 61, ll. 27–30)

This text in section §1, and the similar texts from *Lllor* and on *ysgar* (quoted above), seem to focus on two things: rearing a child involves feeding him, or at least providing for him; and the mother's role is limited to the first year (or year and a half) of his life, calculated from conception and including the time spent in the womb, and she is then not involved.

1.4   **Odyna y tat a dyly keissaѵ idaѵ y holl gyfreideu** 'after that the father is to seek for him all his needs'. This is what happens after the mother has carried out her part: *odyna*, 'after that', 'from then' (*GPC*, 'oddyna'). The father is to provide for the son and what he is to provide is listed.

yn gyntaf y dyry dauat a'e chnuf ac a'e hoen genti 'first he is to give a sheep and its fleece and its lamb with it'. *Dyry* is the 3 sing. pres. ind. of *dyroddi*, 'to give', from *rhoddi*, which is used in ModW. *Dauat*, *dafad*, 'sheep', is f., and this can be seen with the mutations that accompany the f. poss. pron.: *chnuf*, an aspirate mutation of *cnuf*, 'fleece' (*GPC*, 'cnu, cnuf'); and *hoen* with sandhi *h*, from *oen*, 'lamb'. The sheep is to be presented with its lamb *genti*, *ganddi* in ModW, the 3 sing. f. prep. *gan*, 'with'.

1.5 **Ac odyna g⋲eren neu geina⋲c** 'and after that a tallow-cake or a penny'. The *gweren*, 'a piece of tallow', or a tallow-cake, would be a lump of animal fat (tallow) which would be used to make candles. Babies wake in the night, and sometimes need feeding at night: this would provide light.

a phadell hayarn neu pedeir keina⋲c kyfreith 'and an iron pan or four legal pence'. The Iorwerth versions of the Welsh lawtexts along with some others include a lengthy list of equipment and their values for compensation purposes as part of *Gwerth Gwyllt a Dof*, the Value of Wild and Tame (see *LlIor*, §§140–45; *LTMW*, pp. 191–96). In the list of equipment, a *padell haearn*, 'an iron pan', is listed as being worth a penny (*LTMW*, p. 192, l. 29), but this is a more expensive item and worth *pedair ceiniog cyfraith*, 'four legal pence'. This is the full value penny: see above, §1.1.

a muneit o ⋲enith y ⋲neuthur i⋲t ida⋲ 'and a large handful of wheat to make porridge for him'. The word *muneit* refers to as much as can be held in two hands together and so is a large handful (*GPC*, 'munaid'). *Gwenith*, 'wheat', is in contrast to the *yd*, 'corn', which the villein mother would receive, see above, §1.1. Wheat was considered to be better in status, but was also finer in texture. The baby would need a small amount once he progressed to solid food, in the form of *i⋲t*, *uwd*, 'porridge' or 'pap', a sloppy mixture made from wheat and a liquid such as milk or water. The Irish laws on fosterage specify the type of porridge which children of various ranks were entitled to (Anderson, '*Urth Noe e Tat*', p. 2).

a charreit deu ychen o gynnut 'and a two-ox car-load of firewood'. This is a larger vehicle, drawn by two oxen, which means that there is a fair amount of fuel, *cynnud*, coming. See also §1.1 on *carreit* and §6.3 on *cardych⋲el*. This seems to be for the son, as it is listed between other items which are specified as being for the baby; there is also a reference to firewood with the payments to the mother too, see below, §1.6.

a d⋲y gyfelin o vrethyn g⋲yn neu vn brith ar y mab 'and two lengths of white cloth or a speckled one on the son', using the prep. *ar*, 'on' or 'on top of', in the sense of wearing the cloth (*GPC*, 'ar¹' j). The length, *cyfelin*, is measured by a forearm — from the elbow, *elin*, to the wrist or finger — and so this is a cubit and is around 18–22 inches, doubled in this case.

The cloth, *brethyn*, is probably wool in this period. *Ar y mab* uses the prep. *ar*, 'on' or 'on top of', but clearly refers to the fabric being wrapped around the baby. The fabric would be for keeping the child warm, and could refer to swaddling cloths, clothing, or even nappies for the baby (see also Orme, *Medieval Children*, p. 60). It is unclear why it is specified that this can be *gwyn*, 'white', or *brith*, 'coloured' or 'speckled': the white cloth would be more expensive, but it is not compulsory. The more expensive cloth could be for baptism, and would be a keepsake for the woman rearing the child: there is evidence for this happening elsewhere in Europe.

1.6 **A buch vlith a'e llo** 'and a milch cow and its calf': the cow would provide milk for the mother and the baby, and would have considerable value with her calf too. However, in order to take the milk, the calf would need to be prevented from suckling, and this would involve some effort on the part of the woman receiving the animals (see Fergus Kelly, *Early Irish Farming* (Dublin Institute for Advanced Studies, 2000), pp. 37–41). This cow and calf may have a symbolic significance: the mother and her young given to the human mother and her young.

a thri charreit o ƀenith a heid a cheirch 'and three car-loads of wheat and barley and oats'. It is unclear whether this is three car-loads of each, or three car-loads in total: either are possible. This is going to the mother, and it provides food for her, and a variety of grains; a breastfeeding mother would need extra food and enough nourishment. On grain and cereal cultivation in medieval Wales, see Rhiannon Comeau and Steve Burrow, 'Corn-Drying Kilns in Wales: A Review of the Evidence', *Archaeologia Cambrensis*, 170 (2021), pp. 111–49.

a thri charreit o gynnut 'and three car-loads of firewood'. This is for the mother, and is in addition to the firewood quota which the son receives, see above, §1.5.

1.7 **Os myn y vam, hi a'e keiff oll; onys myn, rother y arall** 'If the mother wishes, she may have it all; if she is not willing, let it be given to another'. *Myn* is the 3 sing. pres. ind. of *mynnu*, 'to want, wish, will, desire, be willing' (*GPC*, 'mynnaf: mynnu, mynnyd'), and Richards translates it as 'if the mother will […] if she do not will' (Richards, *Laws of Hywel Dda*, p. 68, l. 39). The question is what the mother wishes to have or to take, or is willing to do: this most likely refers to the son himself. The goods go with the baby, and the text discusses rearing a child: the mother's choice is whether she is willing to bring up and feed her own child. The child could alternatively be given to a wet nurse, who would breastfeed the infant (Orme, *Medieval Children*, p. 58). A *gwraig llwyn a pherth*, who has had a child from her secret relationship, might pass her son to the father's kindred to rear him; a noble son born within the kindred may be given in fosterage. *Rother*, from *rhoi*, 'to give', is in the subj., but imps. It does not have a particle before it, so it may be imper. As it is imps., the mother is not the one giving the goods (or the baby) to another; there is no pron. here so this may also refer to the child being handed over. If the mother does take on the responsibility for the child, she gets all of the goods listed above: *hi a'e keiff oll*. The form *keiff*, from *caffael, cael*, is in the 3 sing. pres. ind. (*GMW*, §161).

§2

2.1 **Rei yssyd yn pedrussaỽ** 'some are doubtful', 'some are hesitant'. The vb *yssyd* is a relative form of the 3 sing. pres. ind. 'to be', and this is an example of its non-relative use after the subject in an abnormal order clause (*GMW*, §66). The vb *pedrussaỽ*, from *petrus, pedrus*, ModW *petruso*, refers to being hesitant to do something. This section opens with this expression of uncertainty, common in the laws, and found in different forms. It may suggest that the laws — or at least this section — were under discussion at the time, and may point to a teaching purpose for the written texts. Often, sections which are claimed to be debated are 'settled' with a decision, as is the case here: §2.2 has the resolution, according to what the law says (see Sara Elin Roberts, *The Growth of Law in Medieval Wales, c.1100–c.1500* (The Boydell Press, 2022), pp. 76–81).
veichogi 'pregnancy'. The word *beichiogi* here is a noun meaning 'pregnancy, conception; fetus' (*GPC*, 'beichiogi²'). The passage discusses the value of the foetus, but it is done in an impersonal way on the whole, by viewing the pregnancy as being one and the same thing as the foetus itself.
gỽreic 'woman': this is a mature woman, not a virgin, see above, §1.1.
peth a dylyir amdanaỽ 'what is owed for it', 'what is right for it'. *Peth* is an interr. pron. contracted from *pa beth*, 'what [thing]'. On *dylyir* and other forms, see §1.2.
ae 'whether', ModW *ai*, often found in pairs in a construction which gives options, 'either this or that'. This is easily confused with *a'e*, 'and his/hers/its', which has an apostrophe in this edition.
ỽynebỽerth 'honour-price', literally 'face-value'. This corresponds to the word *sarhaed*, meaning compensation for insult, payable for deliberate acts. The form *wynebwerth* is older than *sarhaed*, and it is mainly confined to the Law of Women, for a sexual offence within marriage (*WLW*, p. 220). This may place this text on pregnancy within the remit of the Law of Women — it would be a natural link — and applying *wynebwerth* to damage to a foetus may suggest that this is a violent sexual act against the pregnant mother, but it is not clear. The text states that it is *galanas* that is applied in this case, not *wynebwerth*, which puts the killing of the foetus in the category of homicide rather than injuries and insults.
galanas *Galanas* is a major concept in the laws, and the word is applied to different things: the act of homicide, killing a man; a feud or enmity,

although this sense is rare; and the life-value of a person, or the compensation payment which goes to family members if the person is killed (*WLW*, pp. 202–03). *Galanas* is used in the latter sense here. Our text is missing a crucial clause, found in *LlIor*: *o llegryr*, 'if it is destroyed' — compensation for a foetus would only be needed if the foetus were killed (or, *llygru*, 'ruined'; this is an interesting usage here and may be wider than simply killing the foetus). *Galanas* is paid for a deliberate killing. *Galanas* is left in the original in translations of Welsh lawtexts.

2.2   **Kyfreith a dyꝟeit** 'the law says'. See above, §2.1: when there is discussion or questioning on a particular legal rule, the texts usually settle the matter by stating clearly what the law says, or which procedure is to be followed (Roberts, *Growth of Law*, pp. 76–81; and see also §2.4, below).

pan yꝟ 'that it is', from the conj. *pan*, 'that', and the vb 'to be', *yw*. This is a common construction in MW and is emphatic in sense (*GMW*, §87, and see the final paragraph on the use of '*pan yw*, "that it is"'). It is also often written as one word, *panyw*, in the manuscripts. Aled Rhys Wiliam consistently presents it as one word in *LlIor*.

2.3   **Sef achos yꝟ hynny** 'this is the reason'. Another common construction in the laws, leading from a legal rule or procedure and explaining why it is so. *Sef* is a part., meaning 'this/that is', and *achos* is a n., 'cause, reason'. It is sometimes found as *Sef achos yw*, or even simply *Sef achos*.

yn y tri mis kyntaf 'in/for the first three months'. In the laws, as in modern medicine, pregnancy is divided into three trimesters, and this is the first trimester.

y byd gꝟyn ef 'it will be white'. This description of the foetus by colour in the first two trimesters may be due to the way it appears (*WLW*, p. 204). On medieval ideas about the development of the foetus, see Orme, *Medieval Children*, pp. 13–16.

ac y byd trayan galanas arnaꝟ 'and one-third galanas will be upon it', only a third of the galanas payment is to be applied to the foetus in the first trimester.

perued 'middle', referring to the second trimester here.

y byd rud 'it will be red'. In the second trimester the foetus has developed and may have changed in appearance as its circulatory system develops.

ac y byd deuparth galanas arnaꝟ 'and two parts galanas will be upon it': galanas is divided into thirds, increasing by a third for each trimester.

y byd kyflaꝟn o aelodeu ac eneit 'it will be complete in limbs and life'. The foetus would be fully formed by the third trimester, and the lawyers considered it as having 'life'. The medieval idea of when life entered a foetus was complex (as, indeed, it is today), but there is an implication in this passage that it was seen as a gradual process, reaching completion in the third trimester; a baby born in the third trimester would have a good chance of survival.

44   NOTES

ac y byd galanas cỽbyl arnaỽ 'complete galanas will be upon it', the full galanas payment will be due. Each person's galanas varied according to their status, and the full value of a foetus's galanas is not at all clear, although the next sentence goes on to discuss the possibilities. In the thirteenth century, according to the English lawyer Bracton, the killing of a foetus 'counted as homicide only if the foetus was already formed and "animated", possessing a soul' (Orme, *Medieval Children*, p. 15).

2.4   **Rei a dyỽeit** 'some say', again referring to legal debate, and the fact that the law was open for discussion, although once again a decision is made in the following sentence (Roberts, *Growth of Law*, pp. 76-81, and 87-100).

nat iaỽnach talu galanas gỽr ymdanaỽ noc vn ỽreic 'that it is not more right to pay the galanas of a man for him than that of a woman'. It has been agreed that galanas is to be paid for a foetus lost through the actions of another, but the amount of galanas is under question: a woman's galanas is lower than that of a man. The debate here is about how much galanas is to be paid.

cany ỽys peth yỽ 'because it is not known what it is', in terms of gender, whether male or female. This is a valid argument, although the sex of the foetus is visible from the middle of the second trimester, if the baby is born. This seems to assume that the violence which kills the foetus does not also kill the mother but makes her go into labour prematurely.

2.5   **kanys [iaỽnaf] yỽ barnu yn ol y peth pennaf** 'for it is most right to judge according to the highest thing'. *Iaỽnaf* is missing in this text but is required for the sense: it is present in other versions of the same text. The decision is to take the highest possible galanas, which would be a man's galanas, so for compensation purposes the foetus is assumed to be male. There is no suggestion that this is a general view applied in any other circumstance (see also §9.1-3).

yny vedydyer 'until baptized'. Baptism is the initial acceptance into the Christian faith, where the parent(s) of the baby present it to the church; the baby is accepted by the priest and is marked with water, symbolic of the washing away of the original sin (see Orme, *Medieval Children*, pp. 21-26). Baptism may also be a naming ceremony, and the link between naming and baptism is clear in this passage as it states that the baby's name will not be known until they are baptized. In the Middle Ages, babies would be baptized fairly early on, in the first few days or weeks of their lives. Charles-Edwards notes that until the baby was named it would have the status of a foetus, and naming would also mark the gender of the child, paternity, and membership of a kindred since the name was likely to include a patronymic (T. M. Charles-Edwards, *Early Irish and Welsh Kinship* (Oxford University Press, 1993), pp. 175-76;

see also Nicholas Orme, *Going to Church in Medieval England* (Yale University Press, 2021), pp. 302–14; and Orme, *Medieval Children*, pp. 35–43, and p. 328 on the name and baptism marking the baby's gender).

Eleanor Smith also notes that the baptism and naming of children is a particular feature of the Fourth Branch of the Mabinogi, and specifically deals with the six children's names: in five cases their names are assigned at baptism (Smith, 'Baptism, Kindred, and Incest', pp. 2–3).

2.6 **Canys pob dyn a holer** 'for every man who may be claimed [against]', i.e. if a claim is made against a person. *Holi*, 'to make a claim against', is used as a vb, from *hawl*, 'a right', and it is in the legal sense of formal claims being made against a person. The text uses male pronouns throughout, but this is generally the case in the laws as women did not play much of a role in most legal processes.
a dylyir y holi 'he is subject to a claim [against him]', 'it is right for the claim to be made [against him]'; on *holi* see above.
yn herϐyd y enϐ 'according to his name'. It appears that it is not possible to make a legal claim against a person without being able to name them; indeed, in the formal procedures for affiliating or denying a child, the text makes clear that the purported father must be named. A son's name would have a patronymic, naming his father, and perhaps linking him to his kindred as well. (See also §2.5; and Orme, *Medieval Children*, pp. 35–43.)
ac ny ϐybydir yny vedydyer 'and it will not be known until he is baptized', referring to the name, which would be conferred upon the child at baptism. See §2.5, above.
ac ϐrth hynny y byd ar vreint y beichogi 'and because of that he will be of the status of a foetus'. *Beichogi* here is used to refer to the foetus itself, and until baptism, the baby will still have the status of a foetus: see also §2.5, above.

Braint, 'status', is an important concept in the laws, and every man (and woman) had a status. Galanas and sarhaed compensation payments (see §2.1 and §3.10) were calculated according to status, and every man had one status and only one. The manuscript here reads *veint*, 'the amount', *maint* in MW, so 'he will be of the amount/value of a foetus'. While this is a possibility, all of the other manuscripts have *vreint*, clearly referring to status, so it is likely that this is a scribal error.

2.7 **talu drostaϐ a thygu** 'to pay and to swear on his behalf'. If any legal claims are made against the son up to the age of seven, his father would have to swear on his behalf — make oaths to support his good character, or to acknowledge or deny accusations made against someone — and also pay any compensation due. Later on in the text, it is stated that the son does not take on full legal responsibility, including swearing his own oaths and paying compensation, until he is fourteen years old. This accords with other legal traditions (Orme, *Medieval Children*, p. 329).

na dirϐy na chamlϐrϐ 'neither a *dirwy* nor a *camlwrw*'. There were two fines in the laws. *Dirwy* is the word used in ModW for any kind of fine, but in the laws this was a fixed sum, twelve cows or £3, and it was paid to the king for serious offences against society or against the king — it may originally have been seen as a punishment for causing loss to the king (*WLW*, p. 200, and see also §3.7). The other fine is *camlwrw*, and it is a smaller fine, although also paid to the king, and was the sum of three cows or 180 pence (*WLW*, p. 194).

2.8 **Cany dyly y brenhin am annodeu dim** 'because the king is not entitled to anything for inadvertence'. *Anoddau*, from the neg. pref. *an-* and *goddau*, 'intention, purpose', refers to accidental or inadvertent acts. The king would be entitled to one of the two fines for various things, but in general the laws emphasize intention as the main aspect which leads to compensation. The young child here may cause injury or loss to others, and any injury or loss is to be compensated (by his father), but since the son under the age of seven is not considered to have a legal capacity, he is not seen as being responsible for his actions. The sentence goes on to name another man who is in the same category.

dyn ynvyt, ac nat oes bϐyll ganthaϐ ynteu 'a mentally unstable man, and he has no sanity'. *Pwyll* refers to the concept of sanity, or having an ability to reason; the *dyn ynfyd*, 'mentally unstable man', has none. There are several references in the laws to *ynfydion*, including those who have lost their senses due to advanced rabies; they are not considered to be legal persons, and do not have responsibility over their actions.

2.9 **hagen** 'however, but', a word that is used commonly in the laws, usually as a conj. between contrasting statements.

dieissyaϐ y colledic o'r eidaϐ 'restore the loser from what is his', *dieisyaw*, *di* + *eisiau*, 'to not be wanting'. Fines are not paid for the actions of the son under seven years old, but any injury or loss caused by him is to be compensated: the main aim of Cyfraith Hywel is to ensure that in all cases the injured person is compensated so that he is in the same position he was in before the injury or loss occurred. *Eiddo* is a poss. pron. here, meaning 'his', but it develops into a noun in MW meaning 'goods' (*GPC*, 'eiddo¹'; *GMW*, §57).

2.10 **ef ehun bieu tygu drostaϐ a'e tat bieu talu** 'it is for he himself to swear on his own behalf and it is for his father to pay'. Once the child is over the age of seven, he has some legal responsibility, but he has no goods or money, so he swears his own oaths, but his father is responsible for paying any compensation fees which he incurs. *Pieu*, 'to belong to', or 'who has the right (to), who has the duty (to)', is used in the laws in constructions such as this, saying whose duty it is to do something (*GMW*, §88;

and *GPC*, 'piau: pieufod²'). It is usually followed by the action which must be carried out by the person whose responsibility it is.

canys yna y dyt ef y mab 'because then he shall place the son'. *Yna* can mean 'then', as it does here, or 'there', referring to a location — the context usually determines which one is correct. *Dyt ef*, 'he shall place', is the 3 sing. pres. ind. of *dodi*, 'to place'.

a dan laѵ periglaѵr 'under a priest's hand'. *A dan* is the compound prep., *a dan*, or *dan*, meaning 'under'. The *periglawr* is the parish priest or confessor, the priest who would know the person best, and *periglor* and *offeiriad*, 'priest', are interchangeable in some texts (*LAL*, p. 68, n. 83). The word may derive from *perigl*, 'danger', + *awr*, 'time, period' (*GPC*, 'periglor', with a reference to *LAL*, pp. 68–69, which gives the alternative derivation from Latin, *parochialarius*, the priest of the *parochia*, 'parish'). His role in Welsh texts is linked to confession.

This phrase 'go under the priest's hand' is found elsewhere in the laws, and the action may be that of the priest or confessor placing his hand on the child's head in absolution, after he has made his confession before taking his first communion (Huw Pryce, *Native Law and the Church in Medieval Wales* (Oxford University Press, 1993), p. 61). This would occur at the age of seven, according to the laws, and the child would be a full member of the church.

ac y byd arnaѵ gѵed Duѵ 'and God's yoke will be upon him'. The child has been accepted as a full member of the Christian communion, and is therefore 'bound' to God — the phrase uses the metaphor of *gwedd*, 'a yoke', which is used for binding animals together for ploughing, with the image of all Christians labouring together for God.

§3

3.1 **O'r pan aner y mab** 'From when the son is born'. This is likely to be the temporal preposition *o'r*, 'from, since (the time) when' (*GPC*, 'o³' a). Alternatively, it could be a common cond. structure in the laws, perhaps best known from the opening words of the *damweiniau* form (see below, §9.1, and p. 10 above), *O derfydd*, 'if it happens that'. The cond. conj. *o*, 'if', may also take the form *or*, as it has here; it is followed with *pan*, the conj. meaning 'when'. *Aner*, 'is born', is the imps. pres. subj. of *geni*, 'to be born'; in the manuscript it is written as *a aner* with the part. *a* before the vb. This is unusual but may be a scribal habit of the scribe of Q, as he uses the same construction when describing the birth of a daughter, see below, §4.2, and also in another text in the manuscript (NLW, Wynnstay MS 36, fol. 113ʳᵃ, l. 23). The other manuscripts do not have this construction, and it has been amended in the text.

yny vo pedeir blѵyd ar dec 'until he is fourteen years of age'. *Yny, hynny* (and other variant spellings), 'until', is here followed by the 3 sing. pres. subj. of 'to be', *bo*. Boys were deemed to become men and full legal persons at fourteen (Orme, *Medieval Children*, p. 329).

ẅrth noe y tat literally 'at his father's platter'. This particular phrase is only found in the laws, and in this section on children and childrearing. *Noe* is also found in the laws, in the list of equipment, and is translated as 'platter' or 'dish' (*LTMW*, p. 368; *LlIor*, p. 159). *GPC* gives the meaning '(wooden) vessel used in making butter, kneading dough, salting pork &c., shallow dish, bowl, pan, basin, laver, wooden trough'; the phrase here is explained as 'bot wrth noe: ?to be dependent upon' (*GPC*, 'noe'). The basic meaning of *noe* as a platter or vessel clearly linked to food might explain the figurative use: the child 'at his father's platter' is dependent upon him for everything. Owen notes that 'It is difficult to establish precisely the degree of metaphor with which *wrth noe y t(h)ad* ("beside his (or her) father's plate") should be translated' (*WLW*, p. 8).

a'e dat yn arglẅyd arnaẅ 'with his father as his lord', literally 'and his father as the lord upon him'. The son will not be answerable to any other authority at this point.

ny dyly vot arnaẅ cosp neb namyn hẅnn y tat 'there is to be upon him the punishment of nobody except for that of his father'. Again using *dyly* referring to a rule, only the boy's father is to punish him. This can be interpreted more broadly as he is not legally competent at this point. The age of criminal responsibility varied but it was fixed at fourteen in medieval England (on the legal status of children see Orme, *Medieval Children*, pp. 321–27).

namyn ar vn geinaẅc namyn a vedho y tat 'except on one penny except on that which his father controls'. *Namyn*, 'except', occurs twice in this phrase, but there seems to be a case of eye-skip here, with the previous phrase *namyn hwnn y tat*, 'except that of his father'. The text in *LlIor* reads *ac ny dele un keynnyauc o'e da en henne o amser namen a uedho e tat*, 'and he is not entitled to one penny of his goods in that time except that which his father controls' (*LlIor*, §98/1). The first part of the sentence, stating that he is not entitled to (have) any of his goods, is missing in this text, and instead the 'exceptions' are repeated. The father's lordship over his son is extensive and any potential goods or property which the son may have are to be in the control of his father, *a vedho*, from *meddu*, 'to control', again in the 3 sing. pres. subj. Medieval English children were not considered as having property of their own until their teens, and their parents had full responsibility over them (Orme, *Medieval Children*, p. 321).

3.2 **Ac ny dyly vot marẅty arnaẅ** 'and there is not to be a dead-house upon him': he is not subject to dead-house, the concept would not apply to him at his death. The *marwdy*, 'dead + house', is not explained in detail in the laws but there are several references to the term. From the context it is clear that if a man dies without an heir, all of his goods — the house and its contents, and even including food and drink within — go to the lord, although some of the foodstuffs go to the king's officers, e.g. the *rhingyll* ('serjeant') gets the opened meat and butter, the lower stone of the quern, green flax, the lowest layer of corn, the hens and the cats, and the fuel axe inter alia (*LTMW*, p. 34). For the *rhingyll*, this is a mocking entitlement, as Robin Stacey has demonstrated, and the *rhingyll* is reduced to the level of a child (Robin Chapman Stacey, *Law and the Imagination in Medieval Wales* (University of Pennsylvania Press, 2018), pp. 116–25). As the son has no lord other than his father, and his goods are controlled by his father, any property which he may have had would be inherited by his father.

namyn bot yn eidaʋ y tat y holl da 'except that all his goods are the possession of his father'. The word order in this sentence has *y holl da*, 'all his goods', at the end, because it depends on *bod*; literally 'except that it is in his father's possession all his goods'. This, and the remaining part of the sentence, re-emphasizes that the son's father is his lord in this time, *yn hynny o amser*.

y dyly atteb drostaʋ o pob peth 'he is to answer on his behalf in all things', returning to the similar statement in the previous section on pregnancy (see above, §2.7–10), where the father is responsible for his child up to the age of seven, but after that the child swears his own oaths.

3.3 **o'r byd** 'if it is', with the cond. conj. followed by a vb in the habit. pres. ind. used for a fut. sense, as it is an uncertain future occurrence. *Byd* is a MW spelling of *bydd*, the 3 sing. habit. pres./fut. ind. of the vb *bod*, 'to be'. The first part of this sentence expresses what should happen should the boy's father die: 'if it happens/if it is the case/if it is that the father dies'.

y vlʋydyn gyntaf y ganer y mab 'the first year in which the boy is born', with *ganer* as the imps. pres. subj. of *geni*, 'to be born'. It is assumed that the text refers to the child's first year, up to his first birthday, rather than the calendar year in which he is born.

ef ehun yna a a ymreint y dat 'he himself will then enter into his father's status', he will take his father's status, *braint*. This *braint* was hierarchical, and this would mean that the son's life-value would be the same as his father's. Certain payments were dependent on a person's *braint*. The sentence sees the son acquiring this status — he enters into it, *a a* (with the single letter *a* taking two different functions: as the pvbl part., and as the vb *mynd*, 'to go', 3 sing. pres. ind.). The form *ymreint* is the prep. *yn* + *braint*, showing the nasalization which occurs — in ModW, *ym mraint* — but which often caused problems for medieval scribes and writers, and forms such as *ymreint* are common (see *GMW*, §25). The refl. pron. *ehun*, 'himself', is also a contracted form, and is often presented as one word, but in ModW it is written as two words, *ei hun* (*GMW*, §98). The refl. pron. following the personal pron. *ef*, giving the sense of 'he himself', is emphatic (see also §3.5; and *GPC*, 'hunan²' a).

3.4 **ebediỽ** 'death duty', payable to the lord on death. This is different to *marwty*, 'dead-house' discussed above: it was a fixed sum, varying according to status.

3.5 **Gỽedy del ef ymreint y tat, ehun a'e tal** 'once he has entered into his father's status, he shall pay it himself'. Here the refl. pron. *ehun* is used without the dem. pron. *ef*, 'he'.

3.6 **ym pen y pedeir blyned ar dec** 'at the end of his/of the fourteenth year': *y* may be the poss. pron. 'his', or the def. art.; mutations expected in ModW are not always shown in MW, but it is likely to be the first option (although see *LTMW*, p. 131, l. 9). When the boy turns fifteen his status changes. See also §1.2 and §3.1, above.

dỽyn y vab at yr arglỽyd a'e orchymyn idaỽ 'take his son to the lord and commend him to him'. This presentation of the son to the lord, with *orchymyn* meaning 'to commend' or 'to entrust', cf. also 'recommend', may show Anglo-Norman influence, particularly with the homage in the next phrase. Later on in the text, §3.12, there is reference to the son becoming a knight (see Charles-Edwards, *Kinship*, p. 176). This also indicates that the son and father are high status, a *breyr* according to Jenkins (*LTMW*, p. 273). On *breyr* see below, §3.12.

3.7 **Ac yna y mae iaỽn idaỽ** 'and then it is right for him to', a common construction in the lawtexts, giving instructions on what is to be done.

gỽrhav y'r arglỽyd 'pay homage to the lord', which is familiar in Anglo-Norman texts but less so in medieval Wales; Charles-Edwards notes that this is the commendation of the son to the lord, but it is not a feudal commendation (Charles-Edwards, *Kinship*, p. 176). This is one of only two references to homage in the lawtexts, with the other in the Law of Women in a section which is very similar to this, on the presentation of a son at the age of fifteen. The word *gỽrhau* only occurs in the Iorwerth texts, and there is a third example in another text linked to Iorwerth, *Llyfr Damweiniau* (see Introduction, pp. 16–18). The Iorwerth texts, which were created by professional lawyers and scholars in thirteenth-century Gwynedd, during the reign of Llywelyn ab Iorwerth, may have been open to influences from England and Anglo-Norman laws in a way that the more workaday Blegywryd texts and the earlier Cyfnerth texts were not. Charles-Edwards states that this reference is an acknowledgement of the English practice, but 'the foreign status of knighthood has been neatly assimilated to native categories. The *marchog* "knight" is only the *uchelwr* under a new name' (Charles-Edwards, *Kinship*, p. 176).

a bot ỽrth vreint yr arglỽyd 'will be according to/dependent on the lord's status'; as a man, his status is no longer defined by his father, but by his lord.

3.8 **ehun a dyly vot drostaƀ** 'he is to be on his (own) behalf'. Several of the other versions read *ef ehun*, making it clear that it refers to the son rather than the father or the lord. Other texts also have *byeu atteb*, 'is to answer', rather than *a dyly vot*, and it is clear from the context, and the following phrase, that the son is to answer for himself. (See *LlIor*, §98/5.)

am pob peth ar a holer idaƀ 'on everything which is claimed to/against him', *holer* as the imps. pres. subj. of *holi*, 'to claim', see above, §2.6. Here *ar* is not the preposition but the demonstrative pronoun (*GMW*, §75).

3.9 **y vaeddu** 'beat him'; the father is no longer allowed to beat his son now that he is a man. It seems that he was permitted to beat him before he came of age. A man was also permitted to beat his wife in certain circumstances (*WLW*, p. 52; and *LlIor*, §51/3).

mƀy noc estraƀn 'no more than (he would) a stranger'. Physical violence against others is generally not permitted in Cyfraith Hywel, and a man is not allowed to beat his grown son any more than he would a 'stranger', *estron*. Foreigners in the law are generally referred to as *alltud* (lit. 'from beyond this land'), with sections of the lawtexts discussing their rights and status, but *estron* is used in a more general sense to mean a stranger, someone unrelated to the father, not necessarily a foreigner.

3.10 **ac os maed** 'and if he beats him', *maedd* as 3 sing. pres. ind. of *maeddu*, see above, §3.9, with *os* as the object of the verb (see also *GMW*, §272 (b)(2), on *o* with the inf. pron. *'s*).

gan gƀynaƀ ohonaƀ 'and he complains', the son doing the complaining as the prep. *o* in *ohono* marks the subject of the v.n. *cwyno*, 'to complain'. A *cwyn* in the laws is the term for the formal statement which states the legal case and opens proceedings (Sara Elin Roberts, 'Plaints in Welsh Mediaeval Law', *Journal of Celtic Studies*, 4 (2004), pp. 219–61 (pp. 220–22)). In this case the son may complain to others that his father has beaten him (cf. *LTMW*, p. 131, 'complains of him'), but it could equally be read as the son could initiate the formal legal process, 'and he makes a plaint' — the next phrases suggest that it is the latter sense.

ef a ƀna iaƀn idaƀ 'he is to make right to him', the father is to settle the process in a legal manner and make right; *iawn* can mean compensation in some cases, and it is clear that this is one such case.

sarhaet no translation, but *sarhaed* refers to the compensation for a deliberate act, and the act itself (*WLW*, p. 216). Here it refers to the act. The compensation for the deliberate act would be paid in addition to any other compensation for injury, and the amount of sarhaed due varied according to status. See also *wynebwerth*, §2.1.

ac a vyd dirƀyus 'and he will be liable to a fine'. The *dirwy* fine was the higher of the two fines in Welsh law, payable to the lord, see §2.7. The *dirwy* would be applied to anybody committing violent acts against others, and it would be paid in addition to any compensation to the injured person. It is clear that beating his son, who is of age and therefore a man, is an unlawful act which would require compensation if the son speaks out.

3.11 **ac na bo etiued idaѵ** 'and that he has no heir', with *bo* the 3 sing. pres. subj. of *bod*, 'to be'. The word *etiued*, 'heir', does not occur as often as would be expected in the laws; in general the word *mab*, 'son', is used, as women could not inherit land.

yr arglѵyd a dyly y da yn gѵbyl 'the lord is entitled to all of his goods', *yn gѵbyl* meaning 'entirely, the whole, total, all'. The son is no longer under his father as he has been presented to the lord.

yn lle mab idaѵ 'in the place of a son to him': the boy has died without an heir, so the lord becomes the equivalent of a son, i.e. he inherits all of the boy's property as if he were his son. The prep. *i* (*y* in MW), here in 3 sing., can denote possession (*GMW*, §221(d)).

marѵty 'dead-house', see above, §3.2. This passage explains the concept of dead-house: the lord inherits all the goods of a man who has no heir.

3.12 **o'r oet hѵnnѵ allan** 'from that age on', *allan* being '(from then) on' (*GPC*, 'allan³' a), referring to the son, from the age of fourteen onwards.

vn vreint 'of the same status', see §2.6, above, for *braint*, 'status'.

bonhedic kanhѵynnaѵl 'innate nobleman', or a man of known stock; *bonheddig* is the adj. from *bonedd*, 'lineage' or 'origin' (*LTMW*, p. 318; it can also be a n., see *GPC*, 'bonheddig', where the meaning in the laws of 'free Welshman of noble lineage' is noted). The *bonheddig canhwynol* was a freeman, born of a Welsh mother and Welsh father, but his status was not dependent on land. The *breyr*, a nobleman, was higher in status: he was 'a freeman who has come into his patrimony in land because all his ancestors in the direct male line are dead', which the *bonheddig canhwynol* has not done but may yet do (*LTMW*, p. 320; see also *WLW*, pp. 192–93).

canyt oes vreint idaѵ namyn y voned 'for he has no status except for his ancestry/lineage': the *bonheddig canhwynol*'s status is not dependent on land or inheritance.

nat a ynteu 'and he shall not enter into', referring to his father's status; he does not inherit, or enter into, his father's status until his father has died. The neg. conj. *na* takes this form with a /d/ (*-t*) as it is before a vowel, *a*, the vb *mynd*, 'to go', in the 3 sing. pres. ind.

marchaѵc 'a knight'. This is the only use of the word *marchog* in the laws, and this may be an addition to the text following Anglo-Norman influence; it certainly ties in with the discussion on homage and the lord, see above, §3.7. The entire sentence has the air of having been modified or added later to the text: occasionally such revising can be seen in the laws in sections which are written oddly (cf. Pryce, *Native Law and the Church*, pp. 104–05, for an example of a text which may have been revised; and *LAL*, p. 174, where Charles-Edwards suggests that a part of a text on contracts 'has taken an old rule [...] and reinterpreted it as if it expressed current law'). This section is not badly written, but it includes a unique word in the laws, *marchog*.

yny ysgynno 'until he ascends'. This seems to be stating the obvious: nobody can be a *marchog* (lit. 'horseman, horse-rider') until he has ridden a horse. It makes little sense, and may well be an indicator that this has been added to an earlier text and shows Anglo-Norman influence (*LTMW*, pp. 272–73; and see above, §3.7). *Ysgynno*, from *esgyn*, may mean 'to mount a horse' (*GPC*, 'esgynnaf, ysgynnaf' d), but the basic meaning is 'to rise, ascend' (*GPC*, 'esgynnaf, ysgynnaf' a). The alternative interpretation therefore is to link this to the previous statement about entering into his father's status — he may be literally 'ascending into his father's status' — and so the section may be saying that nobody can become a knight unless and until he has taken his father's status after his death.

§4

4.1 **Merch** 'a daughter', or 'a girl'. See *gϐraig*, above, §1.1.

ϐedy bedydyer 'after she is baptized', using the imps. pres. subj. of *bedyddio*. The opening of the section on daughters is similar to that on sons, and follows the same pattern. On *bedyddio*, 'baptism', see §2.5.

yny seith mlyned hyt pan vo 'until she is seven years old'. The construction of the sentence here is different to most of the other versions, which have *ene uo seyth mluyd* or similar (*LlIor*, §99/1), and there may be some corruption of the text in this version, as the sentence order is very unusual. Literally, the sentence reads 'until/in her seven years, until she is'.

ny dyly mynet yn llϐ 'she is not entitled to make an oath', or, literally, because of *mynet*, 'to go', it has the sense of 'enter into an oath'. On oaths, see *talu drostaϐ a thygu*, above, §2.7.

4.2 **O'r pan aner yny vo deudec mlϐyd** 'from when she is born until she is twelve years [old]', see §3.1. Puberty for girls was seen to happen at around twelve, and the church allowed girls to marry at that age (Orme, *Medieval Children*, p. 329).

y dyly vot ϐrth noe y that 'she is to be at her father's platter', see §3.1.

4.3 **O hynny allan y daϐ bronneu a chedor arnei** 'From then on breasts and pubic hair will come upon her', or '[...] breasts will come and pubic hair on her'. It is not clear whether *y daw*, 'there will come', and *arnei*, 'upon her', are linked; the first may refer to the breasts, and the second to the pubic hair, but they could both refer to both things. Physical symptoms of puberty are not specified for a boy, but in the case of a daughter these would be signs that her body was maturing, and she would be ready to bear children and thus be given to a husband.

blodeua 'menstruates', although the word literally means 'to flower', or 'to bloom'. This sense appears to be limited to the lawtexts (*GPC*, 'blodeuaf' b).

ac yna y byd oet idi y rodi y ɼr 'and then she will be of an age to be given to a husband', although *y byd oet idi* may mean 'will be time for her', with *oed* taking the sense of a point in time or appointed time, rather than her age from birth. See also *o'r oet hɣnnɣ allan*, above, §3.12.

vedu yr eidi 'control what is hers', and see above, §3.2, §3.8. A woman had very limited property rights, so it can be assumed that this is simply a mirroring of the equivalent section on sons.

4.4 **Kynny chaffo hi y rodi y ɼr** 'although she is not given to a husband', she remains unmarried. *Kynny* is the neg. of *kyn*, 'although', as a combination of *kyt* and the neg. part. *ny* (*GMW*, §262). *Caffo* is the 3 sing. pres. subj. of *caffael*, 'to have', used in the passive here.

onyt hi ehunan a'e mynn 'unless she herself wishes it'. The young girl appears to have relative freedom of choice in this passage, and she may stay with her father if she wishes, or go elsewhere with her property. The problem is that she has limited options, and it is rather uncertain where she would go or how she would live: this may be a hidden warning that it is better for a girl to marry (Roberts, '"Gwreic wyf fi"', p. 30). In this text, it is clear that it is the daughter's wish, *hi ehunan*, 'she', with the dem. and refl. pron. together; in the text in *LlIor*, it is her father's wish: *ef ehun* (*LlIor*, §99/4).

amobyr A word which has no English equivalent and is left untranslated in editions of the laws, this was the payment to the lord when a woman was married for the first time, a 'virginity payment' (*WLW*, p. 190). It was payable by the father, if he was his daughter's 'giver', in a 'gift of kin' (formal lawful) marriage. The text may be corrupt here, and it gives a different reading to other versions such as in *LlIor*: here it states that the father only pays amobr *onyt ehun a'e mynn*, 'unless he wishes to do so', which is unusual, as it was not an optional payment. This may be a case of eye-skip, with the same words on the previous line, and the remainder of the sentence, *o'e vot yn rodyat arnei*, 'because he is her giver', may be an attempt to make good the error: if the father is his daughter's giver, he is bound to pay her amobr.

4.5 **Os ynteu ehun a'e ryd hi** 'If he gives her himself'. This is a different version of the text to that in *LlIor*, which states that every girl's bestower pays amobr for her. This text may be corrupt, and it is not entirely clear to whom *ehun*, 'himself', or possibly 'herself', is referring: it could be the father, but it could be an attempt to say that the girl is giving herself in marriage.

kymeret veicheu y gan y neb a'e kymero 'let him take surety from whoever takes her'. *Meichiau*, 'surety, security', is the act of taking security from others in any kind of legal contract; the *mach*, 'surety', was a man who ensured that everybody carried out their part in a contract (*WLW*, pp. 210–11; *LAL* is a study of the Suretyship tractate and has very detailed notes on the concept and the various uses). *Y neb a'e kymero*, 'whoever takes her', is the husband, and it is uncertain what is happening here: the person giving the woman is to get a surety (a guarantee that something will be done) from the bridegroom or his family. This is likely to be a way of ensuring that the amobr will be paid one way or another. In *Ll Ior*, the text states, 'every bestower of a woman is bound to pay her amobr unless he takes sureties for paying it from him to whom she is given' (*LTMW*, p. 132), and this text may be a version of the same thing. The situation may be that the father is not the girl's giver, i.e. it is not a 'gift of kin' marriage, but the amobr still needs to be paid, and this falls to the new husband. The father — presumably — needs to ensure that it is paid, and so he should organize a surety as a guarantee.

4.6 **y dyly vot heb veichogi** 'she should not be pregnant'. The preposition *heb*, 'without', is used with the v.n. to express the neg. (*GMW*, §183(b)). A girl was not allowed to become pregnant during this time, between the ages of twelve and fourteen (or the end of her fourteenth year).

odyna 'after that', see §1.4, above.

deugeint mlyned 'forty years', two twenties in the vigesimal system.

ymdḃyn 'to conceive, to become pregnant'. This refers to the lawtexts' view of a woman's fertile years, which end at the age of forty.

nyt a galanas arnei 'galanas will not fall upon her', meaning that she would not be expected to pay galanas, the life-value of a person killed by another. The father and mother of a homicide pay a large part of the galanas payment (*LTMW*, p. 144), but the galanas rules also state that women and clerics are exempt from paying galanas if 'they deny that they will ever have children' (*LTMW*, p. 147).

na llṽ heuyt pryt na bo plant idi 'nor an oath also since she will not have children': *heuyt*, 'also', has been added for emphasis. She does not pay galanas, but she does not need to swear an oath either; *pryt ... na* is a neg. conj. meaning 'since ... not, seeing that ... not' (*GPC*, 'pryt¹' conj. b): now that she is over forty, she will not have children.

diheu vyd yna 'it is certain then', *diheu* formed of the neg. pref. *di-* and *-heu*, as in the second element in *amau*, 'to doubt' (*GPC*, 'diau¹'). According to the laws, a woman is not expected to conceive after the age of forty.

§5

5.1 **Pwy bynnac a vynno** 'whoever wishes', with *mynno* as the 3 sing. pres. subj. of *mynnu*, 'to want, to wish'. This is a common opening to a section of law, and several well-known tractates or sections open with *pwy bynnag*.

gwadu mab yn gyfreithawl 'deny a son legally'. The formal process of denying a son from a kindred — along with the process of accepting a son into a kindred — is found in all the versions of the laws in different forms. It occurs as a triad, or sometimes a pair of triads, in Cyfnerth, Blegywryd, and the Latin texts (*LT*, pp. 60–63, 132–33, 261–62), but the section in Iorwerth is expanded, and may well have been reworked from an earlier text more similar to that found in the other versions. The opening words of the section refer to denial, but the focus of the section is quite clearly on acceptance, or affiliation, of a child into a kindred.

yny dycker yn gyfreithawl gysseuyn 'until he is first legally affiliated', with *dycker* as the imps. pres. subj. of *dwyn*, 'to bring' or 'to lead' (*GPC*, 'dygaf: dwyn¹'; the legal sense of affiliation into a kindred has been given a sub-category, b). The use of *yn gyfreithiol*, 'legally', shows that this is a formal process. In general *yny* means 'until', but the use of the subjunctive implies that this may not happen, and 'unless' would be an appropriate English equivalent. See also §9.9.

canyt reit y neb atteb yn annolo 'because nobody needs to answer uselessly', *rhaid* used in the sense of 'there is no need to/for anybody'. The word *anolo*, translated as 'irregular' by Dafydd Jenkins, has different senses, with *GPC* offering 'worthless, useless, null and void', when it is used adjectivally (*GPC*, 'anolo'). Here, it means 'in a useless way': if the formal legal process is not followed — e.g. the man answers to a claim of paternity made in a casual way — the answer would be futile. It is explained in the next clause.

anolo yw pob peth ny bo kyfreithawl 'everything which is not according to law is useless'. The formal process is then outlined.

5.2 **Pa wreic bynnac** 'whichever woman'. *Gwraig* is used here as the woman has had a child and is no longer a *morwyn*: see above, §1.1.

dwyn 'affiliate'. Although the word *dwyn* has a basic meaning of 'to bring, to lead', here it is the specific legal sense of affiliating a son into a kindred; see also §5.1.

5.3 **Dyuot hi a'r mab** 'she and the son come', using a v.n. to denote obligation (*GMW*, §181n, pp. 162–63). The mother swears the oath, but her baby son must be present. This would be for proof of his existence, and to show that she is affiliating the specific baby boy and remove the possibility for future doubt or corruption.

yr eglwys y bo y wydua yndi 'the church in which his burial-place is'. This refers to the father's usual parish church, although *gwyddfa* (the unmutated form has a g-) is a complex word. Well known as the name of Wales's highest mountain, Yr Wyddfa, it has various senses, but here it means 'burial-place', or rather the church where the purported father's ancestors are buried, tying in with the sense of the wider kindred and ancestral background (*GPC*, 'gwyddfa'). In the versions in Cyfnerth and Blegywryd, the procedure takes place with a priest or confessor present (*LT*, pp. 60–63, 132–33, 262), and in the procedure for affiliating a child to an alien (see below), it takes place in the church where the father takes his communion.

y llaѡ deheu ar yr allaѡr a'r creireu 'her right hand on the altar and the relics'. Pryce notes that the use of relics in oaths is 'the most obvious demonstration of the supernatural character of oaths in Welsh law', but it is also an aspect which makes Welsh law appear a bit old-fashioned (Pryce, *Native Law and the Church*, pp. 39–44).

a'r llaѡ asseu ar ben y mab 'and her left hand on the son's head'. This process of swearing an oath with the left hand on the thing which is being sworn upon is also common: holding an animal's right ear to swear ownership, or, in accusations of rape, holding the man's penis (Pryce, *Native Law and the Church*, p. 42).

ac velly tygu y Duѡ yn y blaen ac y'r allaѡr honno ac y'r creireu da yssyd arnei ac y vedyd y mab 'and so swears to God first and to that altar and to the good relics which are on it and to the son's baptism'. This oath to assign paternity of her son to a man is placed firmly in the Christian tradition, swearing to God first, showing the seriousness of it. After swearing to God, there is a tripartite division to the oath — the altar, the relics, and baptism — presumably for emphasis but also linking to the spiritual (see Pryce, *Native Law and the Church*, pp. 39–44). The reference to the baptism may be significant in terms of the son's name and identity; see above, §2.5.

na ry greus tat y galhon mam y mab hѡnnѡ 'that no father created this son in a mother's womb'. Using a direct quotation for the words to be used, this is a dramatic statement. The combination *y galhon* is an attempt to represent the nasal mutation of the prep. *yn* + *c*- (see Introduction, pp. 25–26). *Calhon* here means 'womb' or 'belly' (*GPC*, 'calon^1 b') rather than heart — although Jenkins translated it as 'heart', giving the passage a rather romantic air (*LTMW*, p. 132). *Ry greus* is a combination of the affirm. part. *ry* + the vb *creu*, 'to create', in the pret.: 'this particle was commonly employed in the early period, but is less frequent in late MW' (*GMW*, §185). This may point to the passage being older than the earliest manuscripts which contain it. Older forms are often kept in the lawtexts in direct speech, or in proverbial or gnomic phrases.

namyn y gѡr a'r gѡr (erbyn y enѡ) 'except for such-and-such a man (named)'. This text may be a model text, with the temporary words *y gwr a'r gwr*, 'so-and-so', to denote when the father is to be named, and the emphasis that he is to be called *erbyn y enw*, 'by his name' (*GPC*, 'erbyn²' a): the actual name must be used, leaving no room for doubt.

y'm calhon i 'in my womb', *y'm* as the prep. *y*, 'in', with the 1 sing. inf. pron. *'m (fy)* (*GMW*, §222).

5.4 **y Gymro** 'to a Welshman'. This is in contrast with the next section, which discusses affiliating sons to foreigners.

5.5 **alltut** 'alien', the word commonly used in the lawtexts for a foreigner, a man from another land, *all-* as in *allan*, 'outside, beyond', and *tud*, 'land, territory'.

5.6 **yr eglỽys y kymero ef y dyfỽr sỽyn a'e vara offeren yndi** 'the church in which he takes his holy water and mass bread'. Pryce notes that 'the water and bread referred to were not sacraments, but rather blessed elements which were distributed amongst the congregation at the end of the mass, and which were held to have healing and protective properties' (Pryce, *Native Law and the Church*, pp. 58–59). While *offeren* is the usual word for 'mass', the divine office or Eucharist in a church, *dŵr swyn* is holy water (on the use of holy water see Orme, *Going to Church*, pp. 235–37, 247).

megys y dyỽespỽyt vchot 'as was said above', a common phrase in the Iorwerth texts (Roberts, *Growth of Law*, pp. 76–81; and see above, §2.1). The use of *uchod*, 'above', shows that there is a clear sense here that this is a written text; the lawtexts show signs of having an earlier written origin than the extant manuscripts. The form *dywespwyt* is a variant of *dywetpwyt*, imps. pret. of *dywedyd, dweud* (on *-pwyt*, see *GMW*, §135(a)).

5.7 **ae kymryt y mab yn gyfreithaỽl ae ỽadu yn gyfreithaỽl** 'either to affiliate the son legally or to deny him legally', following the legal processes set out here for both options. The second instance of *ae* causes a soft mutation in *gwadu*, because *ae* also contains the 3 sing. m. inf. pron. *'i*.

5.8 **yr eglỽys a dyỽedassam ni vchot** 'to the church we stated above', referring back to the previous section. The process is clearly very similar to the one which the text has just outlined, and there is considerable repetition here with minor changes to the wording to match the context.

y'r gỽr a'e gỽahanỽys ef o gredigaeth tat a mam 'to the man who separated him from the creation of father and mother': the father swears a very similar oath to the one the mother would swear to affiliate the son. The difference here is that he swears that he was not involved in the son's conception — some other man was. The spelling of *gredigaeth*, 'creation', is unusual here: it is normally *creadigaeth* or *creedigaeth*, and it may be that the single *-e-* represents two (*GPC*, 'creadigaeth, creedigaeth').

ac nat oes dauyn o'e ỽaet yndaỽ onyt o Adaf 'and that there is not a drop of his blood in him unless from Adam'. *Dafn*, written with the epenthetic

5.9 **O deruyd idaƲ ynteu** 'If it happens that he'. This is the well-known cond. structure which is the opening words of the *damweiniau* form, *O derfydd*, 'if it happens that'. The cond. conj. *o* is linked to *derfydd*, the 3 sing. habit. pres. or fut. ind. of *darfod*, a compound of *bod*, 'to be', meaning 'to happen' (*GMW*, §154). The words *o derfydd* often open sentences which give a different scenario to the one which has just been discussed.

keissiaƲ oet am y lƲ 'to seek a delay for his oath', *oed* meaning a delay, but also a fixed point of time in the laws (*GPC*, 'oed²' a).

hyt trannoeth 'until the next day' (*GPC*, 'trannoeth').

5.10 **keissiaƲ oet y geissiaƲ creireu** 'seek a delay for seeking relics'. This was one of the permitted reasons to request a delay to legal proceedings: relics were clearly allowed to be fetched and used for oaths in various places (Pryce, *Native Law and the Church*, p. 42). On *keissiaƲ*, see §1.4; *oet*, §5.9; and *creireu*, §5.3.

tridieu *tri + dieu*, 'three days' (*GPC*, 'tridiau, tri diau').

namyn y kymƲt ehun 'except her own commote'. The woman was not allowed to travel far to find the relics but had to do so locally, in her home area. The *cantref* was the larger administrative unit in medieval Wales, similar to the English hundred. *Cantrefi* were divided into smaller units called *cwmwd*, pl. *cymydau*, 'commote' (*LT*, p. 439). Again, *y kymwt* is an attempt to show the nasalization of *cwmwd* after the poss. pron. *y*, 'her'.

§6

6.1 **ny eill hƲnnƲ kaffel tat vyth gƲedy** 'that one may never have a father after that', i.e. the son. He has been affiliated but the process has not worked and he has been denied. The process cannot be repeated to attempt to affiliate him to a different man, for obvious reasons: the mother has already sworn an oath on the relics naming the father. *Kaffel* is the vb 'to get, receive', but it has different stems: *caff-*, *cah-*, and *ca-* (*GMW*, §161). In ModW the form is usually *cael*, but the stem *caff-* remains in use in some forms and in some dialects; *caffael* is used formally in a legal sense or in business for 'procurement'. See also §1.7.

6.2 **y vam a'e dƲc ef yn gyfreithaƲl y tat a'e gƲadƲys** 'the mother has affiliated him legally to a father who has denied him'. This repeats the statement in the previous sentence, that a mother can only attempt to affiliate a child once, to one man. The father has successfully denied that the son is his.

ny eill hitheu y dƲyn ef y dat arall eilƲeith vyth 'and she cannot affiliate him to another father a second time ever'. The laws are keen to emphasize that affiliation is a process which can only take place once; *eilƲeith*, 'a

6.3 **ny byd cardychỽel ynteu byth ar hỽnnỽ dracheuyn** 'he will never be car-returning to him again': the son will not be 'car-returning' to the same father. See the note on *carreit*, §1.1. A *car* refers to some sort of basic vehicle, perhaps with wheels. In the compound *carddychwel* found here, it is combined with the element *dychwel*, 'return'; *cargychwyn, cychwyn*, 'to start, set off', is also known in the laws. Wiliam states that 'the first element in the compound is taken to be *carr*, a cart or vehicle: and the moving of the vehicle is understood as a symbol for leaving home and settling elsewhere' (*LlIor*, p. 110). The reference to the vehicle may mean that this is 'to depart/return in a formal or ceremonial way': the car may represent movement, or perhaps transporting goods, moving house (*LT*, p. 239).

In Welsh land law, *carddychwel* or *cargychwyn* means to return to or depart from one's land, but in a significant and often final way, after following the legal process; *cargychwyn* is also used in the Law of Women, where the woman leaves after separation from her husband. There is also a triad, *Tri chargychwyn*:

> Tri chargychỽyn heb attychỽel: vn yỽ gỽreic gỽedy yd yscarho a'e gỽr yn gyfreithaỽl, a chyssỽynuab gỽedy gỽatter o genedyl y tat yn gyfreithaỽl, a threftadaỽc pan del y dilis gỽedy y bod yn arglỽydiaeth arall; o iaỽnder nyt ymchoel trachefyn.
>
> Three car-startings without return: one is a woman after she has separated from her husband legally, and a putative son after he has been denied from the father's kindred legally, and a patrimonial when he comes to his rightful place after he has been in another lordship; rightfully he should not return afterwards. (*LT*, pp. 142–43, Q104)

The word *cargychwyn* is not found in the Iorwerth texts, but there are three examples of *carddychwel*, and two of them discuss the denial of a son (*LlIor*, §54/6, in the Law of Women, and §100/11, which is the text we are discussing). The other example of *carddychwel* is in the Law of Women discussing a woman who has separated from her husband (*LlIor*, §52/5). In both situations, the person is not permitted to return to a kindred: the woman after separation, and the son after the failed affiliation (he is not allowed to return to the kindred to which his mother attempted to affiliate him). Wiliam also states that 'It is possible, however, that in *karrdychwel* that the first word is *câr* "kindred", and "returning to kindred" seems to be more in keeping with the sense of the context' (*LlIor*, p. 110). This may be relevant in the two examples in *LlIor* but is less so in the Land Law example given in the triad. In *LlIor*, *karrdychwel* is consistently spelled with *-rr-*, which favours taking the first element to be *car(r)*,

second time', is an adverb, and the sentence ends with *vyth*, 'ever', which is very final.

'vehicle'. In this particular case, also in the Law of Women, once the son has been denied (formally, legally) by the purported father, he will never again be able to move into that kindred, at least not by following the formal legal process of affiliation.

kanyt adѵna kyfreith a ѵnel 'because law does not undo what it has done': this phrase has the air of a proverb and is one of the general statements about law sometimes found in the lawtexts. There are two collections of proverbs in manuscript Q, closely linked to the two collections in the Red Book of Hergest, and a version of this proverb appears in those collections, as *Nyt atwna duѵ ar a wnel* ('God does not undo what he has done'), (Richard Glyn Roberts, *Diarhebion Llyfr Coch Hergest* (CMCS, 2013), p. 29). Roberts notes in his study of the proverbs that many of them have a legal air (Roberts, *Diarhebion*, pp. 5–6). The proverb in this text is clearly a version of the proverb in the collections, but with law taking the place of God, and the God version of the proverb was well known and occurs in several medieval Welsh poems, including in Canu Llywarch Hen, the Gogynfeirdd, and Dafydd ap Gwilym (Roberts, *Diarhebion*, p. 95).

6.4 **ѵeithion** an adv., a contraction of *y waith hon*, '(at) this time, this time', and so can mean 'now', for example, in the model pleadings for land, where the justice is to say to the parties *Emdyweduch o keureyth weythyon*, 'Plead now by law' (*LlIor*, §74/1; *LTMW*, p. 85). Here it has the further meaning of 'now', but with a future sense, 'from now on', 'hereafter' (*GPC*, 'weithian, weithion, weithan, weithon, &c.'): this is his new status. **ѵrth genedyl y vam y byd y vreint** 'his status will be according to his mother's kindred'. This is an unusual case, and is contrary to the section discussing the status of the son, above, §3.2. As the son has been denied, he is not linked to any kindred on the male line and so his status must be, unusually, according to the female line.

kenedyl y vam a dal deuparth yr alanas 'the mother's kindred shall pay two-thirds of the galanas'. The fine for homicide, galanas, was divided into three, according to the text in Iorwerth:

> Pvybynnac a uo llowrud, galanas cubyl a dyguyd arnav, ac val hyn y rennyr galanas: trayan ar y llowrud ac ar y tat a'r uam y gyt ac ew o bydan byu. Ac o hynny y deuparth arnau ew, a'r trayan ar y tat a'r uam; o'r trayan a dav ar y tat, duy geynnyauc ar y tat ac un ar y uam.

> Whoever is a slayer, the entire *galanas* falls on him, and *galanas* is divided as follows: a third on the slayer and on the father and the mother if they are alive. And of that, two thirds on him, and a third on the father and the mother; of the third that falls to the father, two pence on the father and one on the mother. (*TCC*, §107.1–2; see also *LlIor*, §106/1–3)

> O'r deuparth a a ar y genedyl, y trayan ar genedyl mam y llowrud a'r deuparth ar genedyl y tat.
>
> Of the two thirds that fall to the kindred, a third is on the kindred of the mother and two thirds on the kindred of the father. (*TCC*, §107.4)

In this case, as the son has no father's kindred, the mother's kindred will be paying two-thirds of the fine: the mother's kindred takes on the parents' share by themselves, and the siblings' share is all taken from the mother's side too.

a'r trayan arnaẅ ynteu y llofrud 'and the third on he himself as the homicide'. The final third will be paid by the son himself, as is usual in homicide payments according to the text in Iorwerth (*TCC*, §107.1–2; *LlIor*, §106/1–3).

kenedyl y vam a dyly deuparth y alanas 'and the mother's kindred is entitled to (receive) two-thirds of his galanas'. If the son is killed, his life-value is paid to his kindred, with the system working in reverse:

> A'r deu parth a a y'r genedyl a rennir yn teir rann, ac o'r hynny traean y genedyl y vam a'r deu parth y genedyl y tat; ac velly y kymerir galanas o draean y traean.
>
> And the two thirds that go to the kindred are divided into three parts, and of those one third goes to the kindred of the mother and two thirds to the kindred of the father, and in that fashion is galanas received, from third to third. (*TCC*, §108.1a)

As there is no father's kindred, the mother's kindred receives the greater part (see also *LlIor*, §106/1; *LTMW*, p. 144).

6.5 **a hẅnnẅ yẅ vn o dri dygyngoll kenedyl** 'and that is one of the three dire losses of a kindred'. *Dygngoll* is formed of the words *dygn*, 'dire', and *coll*, 'loss' (Sara Elin Roberts, 'Tri Dygyngoll Cenedl: The Development of a Triad', *Studia Celtica*, 37 (2003), pp. 163–82 (pp. 166)). The text is discussing potential situations where a kindred would suffer a *dygngoll*, a 'dire loss': someone has killed another man, and so the galanas payment needs to be paid. This would have been a substantial sum, and the responsibility fell on the wider kindred. The first and third examples have situations where the homicide has no father's kindred, and so the full burden for the galanas payment falls on the mother's kindred, leaving them with a serious financial loss. In the second instance, it is the dead man's kindred who may suffer the loss: they have lost a kinsman to homicide, and may also potentially miss out on the galanas compensation because of the killer's status as a doubted son. The section also involves possible manoeuvring and misuse of the affiliation and denial process.

Even though this section is not marked as a triad, the closing sentence notes that it is — or perhaps in the case of this text, was taken from — a triad. This item in the Iorwerth 'triad' is not found in the Blegywryd, Cyfnerth, or Latin versions of the triad, and it may be that the original triad in an earlier text was taken by the Iorwerth redactor and rewritten, keeping one item (the second item in this text in Iorwerth) but finding or creating two similar situations — focusing on the galanas and a doubted son — for the other two. It is interesting that the first and third sections in this text — the 'new' sections, not found in the triad in Blegywryd and Cyfnerth — are similar, with the focus on the mother's kindred paying all of the galanas, and the second item, which is found in the triad, has a different focus. There is a *Tri dygngoll* triad in the *damweiniau* collections which, like this text in Iorwerth, focuses on doubted sons and galanas fines (*LTMW*, pp. 134–35). It is unclear why the triad was not labelled as a triad in Iorwerth (Roberts, '*Tri Dygyngoll Cenedl*', p. 170).

6.6 **Arall yƀ bei darffei** 'another is if it happens', with *darffei* being the imps. impf. subj. form of *darfod*, see *derfydd*, §5.9. This refers to another instance of *dygngoll cenedl*, which may suggest that this was originally a triad, or at least a numerically organized section.

meichiaƀ o genedyl y llofrud ar yr alanas 'surety from the homicide's kindred on the galanas'. The kindred have agreed that a galanas payment is to be paid, and they have given a surety on the payment to guarantee that it will be paid. On *meichiau*, see above, §4.5.

dƀyn o'e vam y llofrud y dat arall 'the mother affiliates the homicide to another father', referring back to the formal process of affiliation, see above, §5. This is a rather unusual situation, since the son has been brought up in a certain kindred, but now that he has killed a man, and the homicide payment has been agreed, the mother decides to affiliate him to another kindred. The focus here is on the homicide payment and who is responsible: the next statement makes it clear who is responsible for paying it. This situation is found in the *Tri dygngoll* triad in the Cyfnerth and Blegywryd texts (Roberts, '*Tri Dygyngoll Cenedl*', p. 169).

pan yƀ y genedyl a veichiƀs ar yr alanas bieu y thalu 'that it is for the kindred who gave surety on the galanas (payment) to pay it'. If the affiliation of the son to a new father is a way of avoiding paying the substantial fine for galanas, the law makes it clear that it will not work: the original kindred, who had given surety, a commitment to pay the fine, are the ones who pay it. This is separate to the affiliation process: this may go ahead, but there is no way of avoiding the galanas payment. On *pan yƀ*, see §2.2; *alanas*, §2.1; and *bieu*, §2.10; *veichiƀs* is the 3 sing. pret. of *meichio*, *meichiaf*, 'to give surety' (on the *-ws* ending see *GMW*, §133(4); and also Simon Rodway, *Dating Medieval Welsh Literature: Evidence from the Verbal System* (CMCS, 2013), chs 6 and 7).

o deu achaƀs 'for two reasons', emphasizing that the original kindred will be paying the galanas: because of his status when he committed the killing, and because of the surety.

o ỽneuthur y gyflauan tra vu ar eu breint ỽy 'for committing the killing while he was under their privilege', i.e. he was a member of the first kindred when he killed the man, and therefore the responsibility for paying the galanas falls to them. The word *cyflafan* for killing suggests a slaughter, and it would not be used for an accidental killing; it is also used for a battle (*GPC*, 'cyflafan¹'). In the laws, *cyflafan* is usually applied to very serious offences, usually involving killing (*GPC*, 'cyflafan¹' c).

o dylyu talu o'r neb a veichỽys 'it is for those who gave surety to pay'. The second reason given states — using *dylyu*, which has a strong sense of something which must be done (see above, §1.2) — that the kindred who gave surety are the ones who will be paying, as by giving surety they committed themselves to paying the galanas and took responsibility for their kinsman's act. Moving him to another kindred will not get them out of paying the fine. The concept is found as a proverb in both of the Red Book of Hergest collections of proverbs, and copied at the end of Q: the proverb occurs twice, *talỽys ry ueichỽys*, and *talỽys a veichỽys* (Roberts, *Diarhebion*, pp. 33, 120, and discussion at p. 104).

6.7 **Trydyd yỽ** 'the third is', a common construction in triads, and this suggests that this section is — or was — a triad (*LT*, p. 7).

o rodir Kymraes y alltut 'if a Welshwoman is given to an alien'. *Kymraes* is the female form of *Cymro*, a Welshman, and the nationality is important in this section. In a formal marriage (see above §4.4 and §4.5), the kindred have given one of their women to a foreigner. This would have repercussions as any male children born to the couple would not have a recognizable Welsh kindred on the father's side.

deuparth yr alanas a daỽ ar genedyl y vam 'two-thirds of the galanas come to the mother's kindred'. As in the first case, the killer does not have a kindred to pay the fine on his father's side, because they are foreigners.

a'r trayan ar y llofrud 'and a third on the homicide', the son who has killed another will be paying a third of the galanas, as is standard, with his mother's kindred paying two-thirds. See above, §6.4.

a hynny ỽrth nad oes genedyl tat a'e talo 'and that because there is no father's kindred who may pay it', *talo* as 3 sing. pres. subj. of *talu*, 'to pay'. See above, §6.4. This part of the text, the third example, is very similar to the first in the section, with the second example perhaps taken from the triad which occurs in Blegywryd, Cyfnerth, and the Latin texts; see above, §6.5, for the discussion on the *dygngoll* triad.

6.8 **A hỽnnỽ a elỽir** 'and that (one) is called'. The dem. pron. *hwnnw* refers to the specific situation outlined in the previous sentence; alternatively, it may refer to the payment called *gwartheg dyfach*.

ỽarthec deuach 'cattle of dark ancestry'. Although there are several suggestions on how to translate this phrase, it is clear that it was one which caused problems for the scribes and compilers. The discussion centres on the elements within the word, and whether the second element is from *mach*, 'surety'. If that is the case, then this could be 'cattle with surety': in his translation of this same section, Dafydd Jenkins offered 'secured cattle', that is, cattle with surety on them, because of 'the explanation offered in the text, which implies that *dyfach* is the suffixless verbal adjective from the adjoining vb *dyfeichiaf*, "give surety"' (*LTMW*, p. 273). However, if the word is interpreted as the neg. *di* + *mach*, then it could mean 'cattle without surety'. The word *difach*, 'suretyless, without surety', does occur in the laws elsewhere, e.g. *Tri da dilis divach*, 'Three valid unsuretied goods' (*LT*, p. 146, S180). *GPC* gives both 'having a surety, ensured, guaranteed' as a translation, but also 'without a surety', although under *gwartheg difach* it is noted that 'the term was sometimes misinterpreted by early scribes as well as by later editors as "cattle without surety"' (*GPC*, 'difach, di-fach', 'gwartheg: gwartheg difach').

However, the phrase also occurs in the Iorwerth texts in the Law of Women, in a section on the child of a Welsh woman and an alien: Jenkins translates it as 'cattle of dark ancestry' there, but explains in the note on this example, 'A different translation is given here because of the explanation offered in the text' (*LTMW*, p. 58, ll. 8–9, and note on p. 273). Charles-Edwards translates the word, in the Law of Women, as 'cattle of dark ancestry', from *dyf*, 'dark' (i.e. the old composition form of *du*, 'black' < *dubo) + *ach*, 'lineage, ancestry' (*WLW*, p. 205). The explanation is that 'the cattle are then of "dark ancestry" because they are paid by the maternal kin of a foreigner's son' (*WLW*, p. 205). The word in the lawtexts is usually spelt *dyf*-, or, in this example, *deu*- (which could either be a simple orthographic variant of *dyf* (/dəv/), or be interpreted as /deu/, the composition form of *dau*, 'two', again referring to the mixed ancestry). The example in the Iorwerth Law of Women is linked to the son of a Welsh woman and a foreign father: 'It is the sons of such women for whom "cattle of dark ancestry" are paid. This is the reason why they are called cattle of dark ancestry, because it is not the kindred of the father which pays them but the kindred of the mother' (*WLW*, Ior §53.3). The equivalent of this section, in the Law of Women, is the only instance of the term in the Cyfnerth texts (see *WLW*, Cyfn §73.30), and the only instance in the Blegywryd texts is a similar section (see *J(ed.)*, p. 74, ll. 1–5). Linking the *gwartheg dyfach* to ancestry, for a child of mixed blood, makes sense. There is little justification for using a different translation for what is clearly the same term in this section in the Iorwerth *dygngoll* section: the scribes' problems with the phrase may have led to attempts at an explanation, which only serves to confuse the matter (*LTMW*, p. 273), but here the translation 'cattle of dark ancestry' still works, despite the following notes in the text itself.

Ϭrth vot yn dir diueichieu ar y gϬarthec hynny 'because it is necessary for those cattle to be suretyless'. There is confusion with the meaning of *diueichiau*; Jenkins, following his explanation of the earlier phrase *gwartheg dyfach*, maintained his translation of 'with surety', and *dir*, meaning 'sure, certain', 'necessary', or 'compulsory'. This is an attempt by the lawbook compilers to explain an old phrase — *gwartheg dyfach* — which had clearly become unfamiliar by the time the earliest Iorwerth texts were being created, but the explanation is not particularly helpful and only underlines the compiler's or scribe's confusion.

canys a gỽarthec y telit pop tal gynt 'because all payments were previously made in cattle'. This is a perhaps botched attempt at clarifying *gwartheg dyfach*, but as Wiliam notes, 'although this is the reason for giving surety for cattle, it still does not explain why this particular payment of cattle should be called *gwartheg dyfach*, for it refers to all payments' (*LlIor*, p. 122). *Telit* is the imps. past subj. of *talu*, 'to pay'.

6.9 **Y deu uab a dyỽedassam ni vchot** 'the two sons which we stated/discussed above'; *dywedasam* is the 1 pl. plupf. ind. of *dweud*, 'to say, to state'. While the text refers to two sons, the section has discussed three scenarios with three sons: one of the three is not being counted. It appears that the one not being counted is the second, the killer whose mother is about to move him to another kindred; in that case, the son already has a father's kindred, and the issue is over who pays the galanas. The other two are more similar in that they have no father's kindred (and the responsibility of paying galanas falls on their mother's kindred): this is clear because the next phrase states what their status is, as this would not be known without a father's kindred. This reference again suggests that the first and third items in this triadic section were new compositions for the text, with the second item taken from a well-known triad, making use of a recognizable phrase (Roberts, '*Tri Dygyngoll Cenedl*', p. 170).

vn vreint ac vn ỽerth ac vn sarhaet ynt a bonhedic kanhỽynaỽl 'they are of the same status and the same value and the same sarhaed as an innate nobleman'. On *bonheddig canhwynol*, see above, §3.12; *braint*, §2.6; and *sarhaed*, §3.10. The section closes by stating the status of the two sons, because as they have no father's kindred, this would not be obvious. All elements of their status are given, but not their life-value, galanas.

§7

7.1 **Mab deolef a vyd** 'there shall be a son by clamour'. *A vyd* is the 3 sing. pres. habit. or fut. ind. of the vb *bot*, 'to be'. The term *mab deolef* is confined to the lawtexts (indeed, to this particular section) and *deolef*, or *dyolef, dolef*, etc., has the element *llef*, 'shout, cry, clamour'. Jenkins has 'clamour'; Wiliam suggests 'outcry' (*LTMW*, p. 134, l. 15; *LlIor*, p. 152). The explanation of the term is given in the next sentence: this is a son who is linked to a particular father because the mother has stated that this is the case, but the formal legal process of affiliation has not been followed. **mab diodef** 'a son by sufferance': the father has treated this son as if he were his own, has 'suffered' him, but again, the legal process has not been followed.

7.2 **mab a dyƀetto y ƀreic ar y thauot leueryd** 'a son whom the woman declares by her word of mouth'. Her declaration is that he is a certain man's son. The phrase *tafod leferydd*, 'tongue + speech', is listed as a term in *GPC* and is found in the laws meaning to state something explicitly; Jenkins has 'by word of mouth' (*GPC*, 'tafod-leferydd'; *LTMW*, p. 134, l. 17).

ac nys dycco y'r dygyn 'and she does not take it to the end point', with *nys dycco* as the neg. 3 sing. pres. subj. of *dwyn*, 'to take': the woman is the one who is expected to take the process to the end. *Dygn* is a noun here, meaning 'the extreme': see also *dygn + coll*, §6.5. The phrase *dwyn i'r dygn* is listed in *GPC*, with the explanation 'to bring to the test, to affirm an oath (the truth of a statement), avow (a statement) as legal evidence' (*GPC*, 'dygn', 'dygaf: dwyn i'r dygn'); it is confined to the laws. Jenkins suggests 'bitter end' (*LTMW*, p. 134). It is the very end of the legal process, followed fully.

hƀnnƀ a ellir y ƀadu pan vynner 'that one can be denied at will', or *pan vynner*, 'whenever it is wished', the imps. pres. subj. of *mynnu*. *Hwnnw*, the dem. pron. 'that one', refers to the boy, who can be denied at any time because the legal process is not complete: the laws are emphasizing the need to follow the full legal process to the end.

7.3 **mab a dycco gƀreic yn gyfreithaƀl** 'a son whom a woman has affiliated legally'. This is the explanation of a son by sufferance: he has been affiliated to a father by his mother, and the full legal process has been followed. **a diodef vn dyd a blƀydyn** 'and he is suffered for a year and a day': this is the son, who has been 'suffered' by the father to whom the mother affiliated him. The father does not have to accept a son affiliated to him; he could deny him, following the legal process, but this has to be done in the fixed legal period of a year and a day. Once that time has passed, the son is accepted and cannot be denied: *ny ellir y ƀadu o hynny allan vyth*, 'he cannot be denied ever from that point on'.

7.4 **ny ellir y ƀadu yn yr yg, kanny ƀadƀyt yn yr ehag** 'he cannot be denied in the rough time, since he was not denied in the calm'. *Yg* has a <g> representing <ng>, /ŋ/ (see the discussion on the orthography of the text in the Introduction, pp. 24, 26), so this is *yng*, or *ing*, which is the first element in ModW *ingol*, 'excruciating, torture'. Here it means 'strait' (as in a narrow and difficult to navigate stretch of a river, commonly used in 'dire straits'), or a rough time, a crisis (*GPC*, 'ing, yng'). The son has committed a killing, which would mean that the galanas payment would fall on the father's kindred: this is a financial crisis (or, indeed, a dire loss: see above, §6.5), and the father suddenly wants rid of him to avoid the financial burden. However, denial is not permitted as a response to a bad period. It is explained that he cannot be denied in a crisis because he did not deny him *yn yr ehag*, from *eang*, 'broad, wide', continuing the imagery of a river to explain the situation, with the good/unproblematic time as a contrast to the crisis, the 'strait'.

ỽrth y vot yn vap diodef 'because he is a son by sufferance': in many ways, this is the real explanation — the previous explanation merely says that someone cannot follow a legal process as a knee-jerk reaction to a crisis. In fact, the son cannot be denied anyway, because he was 'suffered' (which counts as acceptance) for a year and a day, and the time limit for denial has passed.

7.5 **Kyt boet y brenhin a vo tat y vab alltudes** 'Although the king may be the father of an alien woman's son'. This has the appearance of a new law, added to this section. Given that this is the Iorwerth text, created in Gwynedd during the reign of Llywelyn ab Iorwerth (1228–1240), it is a very interesting addition: the princes of Gwynedd were marrying foreign women, and Llywelyn ab Iorwerth himself did just that. If the king denies the son, then the son remains an alien: *alltut vyd y vab o hynny allan*, 'his son will be an alien from then on'. It is not clear why it is stressed that this is the king, and there may be something more behind this statement.

7.6 **Os alltut a ỽatta mab Kymraes** 'If it is an alien who denies the son of a Welsh woman': this is the reverse situation to the king's son with an alien woman. If the alien father denies the child, the child automatically has the status of a *bonheddig canhwynol*, 'innate nobleman' (see above, §3.12), and is in a far better position than his alien father would be. How an alien would be able to follow the legal denial process for Welsh kindreds is a whole other matter.

canys ỽrth vreint y vam y byd pob mab gỽedy gỽatter 'because every son takes his mother's status after he has been denied', a rule which has been explained above, §6.4. *Gỽatter* is the imps. pres. subj. of *gwadu*, 'to deny'.

7.7 **Tat a digaỽn trannoeth gỽadu y mab gỽedy diỽycko y gyfulauan drostaỽ, os myn** 'The father may deny the son the day after, after he has compensated for the killing on his behalf, if he wishes'. This sentence seems to fit better with the opening of the section, not with the previous sentences on denying alien children, as it shares the sentiment expressed in the explanation of the *mab dioddef*, 'son by sufferance': the father may — *a digaỽn*, 'is able to, is allowed to', §7.12 — deny the son *trannoeth*, 'the next day', §5.9, after he has paid compensation for the *cyflafan*, 'killing', §6.6. The word used for paying compensation, or to make reparation, is *diỽycko*, the 3 sing. pres. subj. of *diwygaf*, v.n. *diwyn*, 'to make good, to compensate' (see *WLW*, p. 200; and *LT*, p. 251).

7.8 **rodi da yr meithrin mab** 'gives goods for rearing a son', an action which means that he is committing to rear the child as if he is the father: this is a binding sign of paternity. The goods for rearing a son are detailed in a Blegywryd section, given above, §1.

canys trydyd kymeryat yv ar vab 'because this is one of the three acceptances of a son'. The n. *kymeryat* is 'an accepting, acceptance', from the root of the vb *cymryd*, 'to take'. This phrase, using *trydydd*, 'the third', is used in the prose tales, e.g. the *Mabinogi*, to refer to triads, but is rarer in the laws (see Ifor Williams, *Pedeir Keinc y Mabinogi* (University of Wales Press, 1951), pp. 47, 48, 49, inter alia). There is a legal triad on *Tri chymeryat a vyd ar vab*, 'There are three acceptors of a son', but it refers to the formal affiliation process (*LT*, pp. 184–85, Q186). However, in the *damweiniau*, a text linked to the Iorwerth redaction, there is a triad which discusses the same subject:

> O try mod ny ellyr guadu mab o cenedyl: un ev o'y caffel yn y guely keureythyaul a'y ueythryn ar da gur en dyurthot un dyt a bluydyn. Er eyl ev rody da yr y ueythryn ced boet mab gureyc lluyn a perth uo. E trydyt eu y kymryt en keureythyaul en y uam egluys uel e deweyt keureyth. (*DwC*, 152–54)

> In three ways a son cannot be denied by a kindred: one is, by his being begotten in the legitimate bed and reared on the man's goods for a year and a day without rejection. The second is, giving goods for rearing him even though he be the son of a woman of bush and brake. The third is, accepting him legally in the mother church as law says. (*LTMW*, p. 135)

This may be the triad referred to in this text.

7.9 **y pennkenedyl** 'the head of kindred', a man who 'had a position of some authority over other relatives besides those descended from him' (*WLW*, p. 212). He plays an important role in accepting and denying children into the kindred. The *pencenedl* could be a very important figure, and Charles-Edwards notes that 'there is a striking resemblance between the office of *pencenedl* and that of the king himself' (Charles-Edwards, *Kinship*, p. 203).

ar y seithvet 'as one of seven': it uses the ordinal number to refer to 'one of', in the same way as the reference to the triad, *trydydd cymeriad*, above, §7.8.

vn ved ac y gvattei y tat bei byv 'in the same way that the father would deny him were he alive'. The vb *gvattei* is the 3 sing. past subj. of *gwadu*, 'to deny'; the same ending is used for the 3 sing. impf. ind. In the same way, *bei* is the 3 sing. past subj. of *bod*, 'to be' (*GMW*, §274). This denial is presumably the process described at §5.8, to be done in the same way, the same manner, *vn ѵed* (*GPC*, 'gwedd¹').

a seith gantaѵ o oreugѵyr kenedyl 'with seven (men) with him from the best men in the kindred'. *Gantaѵ* is 3 sing. of the prep. *gan*, 'with', and the head of kindred is to have seven of the *gorau* + *gwŷr*, 'best men', from the kindred with him to perform this ceremony of acceptance. These men are likely to be of the highest standing in the kindred, or perhaps men with no claims against them, and trustworthy men with a good name.

gan y llѵ ѵynt vot yn lan y lѵ ef 'by their oath that his oath is clean', with *lan* as the mutated form of *glân*, 'clean', taking the wider meaning of 'true, honest, sincere', etc.

7.10 **Ony byd pennkenedyl, vn gѵr ar hugeint o oreugѵyr a'e gѵata** 'If there is no head of kindred, twenty-one of the best men deny him'. On the *goreugwyr*, the 'best men' from the kindred, see §7.9. The situation here is where there is no head of kindred — it is uncertain why there would not be one, but it may be that he is not available to perform the ceremony. In that case, more senior representatives from the kindred are needed: twenty-one of them.

7.11 **Herѵyd gѵyr Poѵys ony byd na that na phenkenedyl, dec ѵyr a deugeint a'e kymer ac a'e gѵatta** 'according to the men of Powys, if there is no father or head of kindred, fifty men affiliate and deny him'. The Iorwerth texts of the laws are said to apply to Gwynedd, but there are references to the different methods used in Powys, the neighbouring kingdom (Roberts, *Growth of Law*, pp. 81–84). In Powys it seems that the rules were even more stringent: where there is no father or head of kindred, fifty men from the kindred are needed to carry out both affiliation and denial of a son, considerably more than the twenty-one called for in Gwynedd. Presumably the rules and the numbers were the same in Powys for cases where there was a father or head of kindred. This high number of fifty shows the seriousness of the situation, as finding fifty senior members would be quite a challenge, and it shows that the wider kindred would be involved in this decision: paying a galanas fine would of course affect many people within the kindred. It also gives an indication of how large a kindred could be.

7.12 **Ny digaѵn neb y dygѵydo tir y mab yn y laѵ y ѵadu** 'nobody into whose hand the son's land may fall is permitted to deny him [the son]'. A complex clause, *digaѵn* means 'to be able, to be able to make or cause' (*GPC*, 'digonaf: digoni' b), and is a variant form of *dichon*, 'to be able to' (*GPC*, 'dichonaf: dichon, dichoni'; and *GMW*, §164). The text in *LlIor* has *eill*, from the vb *gallu*, 'to be able to' (*LlIor*, §102/14). This is negative, *ni* stating that nobody is permitted to do the thing stated in the last part, which is *y ѵadu*, 'deny him', referring to the son. The people who are not permitted to deny the son are those who may be able to inherit or get his land. *Digwyddo* is the 3 sing. pres. subj. of *dygwydd*, 'to happen' (*GPC*, 'digwydd¹, dygwydd'), and the land 'may happen' to come or fall *yn y laẃ*, 'into his hand'. Anybody who might be able to get the son's land for themselves is not allowed to deny the son — another explanation that prevents misuse of the denial process.

The text reads *or y dygẃydo* in Q, and also in the related manuscripts J and K, but the *or*, 'if' (*GMW*, §272, *Or*), is difficult to explain here and does not occur in the other versions of the text, which read *y digwyddo* with the pvbl part. *y*. It could also be *o'r y dygẃydo* (*GMW*, §74), but this would also give an unusual syntax. The text has been amended. There are further errors in the next section, and it may be that the original was corrupt at this point.

yr y yrru ohonaẃ 'in order to drive him from it'. This phrase is not found in *Lllor* which has a simpler version, and this may be a case of eye-skip in this text from Q, as the same phrase occurs further down in the manuscript. The version here has been amended, since the form was *yrr*, but this is likely to be a scribal error for *yrru*: the text in J, which shares the same eye-skip, reads *yrru* (*J(ed.)*, p. 123, ll. 39). This is the vb *gyrru*, 'to drive, pursue'; sometimes in the laws it can mean 'to make a claim' (*GPC*, 'gyrraf: gyrru⁷'), but it is the first meaning in *GPC* that applies here, literally driving the son from his land to get it themselves (*GPC*, 'gyrraf: gyrru¹').

braẃt 'brother'. Brothers are not allowed to deny their own brother, presumably because they all share the family land.

keuenderẃ 'cousin'. A cousin may not deny the son with land in order to drive him from it. The text has the same phrase, *yr y yrr[u] ohonaẃ*, further up in §7.12, which may be eye-skip. The phrase itself was problematic and there are various versions in the manuscripts: in *Lllor*, Wiliam amended the text which read *erw*, ?'acre', in B, to *yr eydaw*, 'his possession/goods', from E (*Lllor*, §102/15, n. 4). J and Q are very close at this point, and both share the same reading, which may well be the correct reading: it certainly makes more sense than the alternatives (*J(ed.)*, p. 123, ll. 37–38).

7.13 **gan y llẃ nac yr gobyr nac er gẃerth y maent yn y gymryt** 'by their oath that it is not for a reward nor for value that they are affiliating him'. *Gobr* can also mean 'a fee', and is a variation on *gwobr*, 'reward'; amobr, the virginity payment to the lord in the Law of Women, and above, §4.4, is also linked (*GPC*, 'gobr, gobrwy'). *Gwerth* can also mean 'a price', or even 'a bribe' (*GPC*, 'gwerth'). Some of the son's kindred want to deny him, but others want to affiliate him but may want to do so for reasons of financial gain, even though they have given their oath — *gan y llw*, 'by their oath' — that they are not choosing to affiliate him for gain.

iaẃnnaf yẃ credu 'it is most right to believe', with *iawn*, 'right, proper', used adjectivally, in the spv. It is the ones who are choosing to affiliate him who are the ones to believe, *credu*, despite their possible ulterior motive.

canys gnottaaf yỽ [gỽadu] y mab yr tref y tat 'because it is most usual to deny the son for his patrimony, for the inheritance of his father', i.e. they are more likely to gain (by taking on the son's inheritance) by denying him than they are by affiliating him into the kindred. He may be accepted into the kindred even if some will benefit financially from it; he may not be denied for the same reasons. The text has been amended here with the word *gỽadu* added for the sense — it is there in the sister-text in J (*J(ed.)*, p. 124, l. 4). Manuscript K, from a similar period and which may be linked to Q, has *Canys gnaỽtaf yỽ gỽadu map er tref i tat*.

The word *gnottaa* (as it appears in the manuscript) is also problematic: in *Lllor* the form in Iorwerth B and E is *gnotaw*, with the final <w> seemingly representing /v/ (*Lllor*, §102/16). This is perhaps an example of the loss of the final *-f* (*GMW*, §10). Both J and Q have a similar form — *gnotaa* or *gnottaa* respectively — and it may be that their exemplar had this form, perhaps reflecting the pronunciation with the loss of *-f*; it may have been difficult for the copiers. In this edition and in *J(ed.)* the text has been amended to *gnotaa[f]*; the *-aa* form shows that the *-a* is long. This is the form found in Iorwerth E, *gnottaf*. *Gnotaf* is an adj., in the superlative here, meaning 'to be most accustomed to', 'to be most usual', from *gnawd*, 'usual' + the spv. *-af* with provection (*GPC*, 'gnotâf: gnotáu').

Tref tad, *tref* (lit. 'township', but more likely to mean 'home', see *GPC*, 'tref' b) + *tad*, 'father', means 'patrimony', and the noun *treftadaeth*, 'patrimony', is the same.

7.14 **rac rannu da y mam a'e that a hi** 'against sharing her father and her mother's goods with her'. The wording in *Lllor* is different: *pan ranner da y mam neu y that*, 'when the goods of her mother or her father are shared', and it makes more sense, particularly with *ny ellir*, 'it is not possible', at the end of the sentence. *Rac*, *rhag* here means 'against', but can also mean 'for fear of, in case of; lest' (*GPC*, 'rhag' 5); it does not read as well with *ny ellir*, as the caveat is at the start, in *rhag*. It is clear from this section that the daughter has a share of the goods, they are shared *a hi*, 'with her', specifically. This is the one case where a brother cannot deny his own sister: again, it is for potential financial gain as he could take her share once she has been denied. It is interesting that a daughter can be denied at any time otherwise, but perhaps it is unlikely since a girl will have no real role in the kindred, and the entire process focuses on denying a son, rather than a daughter.

7.15 **Ac velly pop alltut a digaỽn gỽadu** 'and in the same way every alien can deny'. Like the daughter, aliens do not play a major role in a kindred and so they may deny their own siblings, except if it is likely to be done for financial gain.

rac kyfuranu o da eu mam a'e tat ac ѵynt 'unless it is against sharing the goods of their mother and father with them'. *Cyfrannu* can mean 'to share', but here it is clearly being part of the sharing, and *rhag*, 'against', is neg. (see §7.14): they are preventing their sibling from getting a share, and taking the share of the goods for themselves by denying them from the kindred.

neu rac diѵc eu kyfulauan a ѵnelѵynt 'or against compensating for the killing which they might commit', *gwnelwynt* as the 3 pl. pres. subj. of *gwneud*, 'to do, to commit' (*GMW*, §141). On *diwc* see §7.7; and on *cyflafan*, see §6.6.

§8

8.1 y tat ehun 'the father himself', a standard form of words, but in Q the manuscript reads *y tat eu hun*, which seems to have *eu* as poss. 3 sing. and poss. 3 sing. *y* without the following lenition. This may be an error in Q, and its sister-manuscript, J, has the more usual *ehun*, so the text has been amended here. Both fols 86ᵛ and 87ⁱ in Q are untidy and smudged, with a different hand appearing for the first ten lines on fol. 87ʳᵇ, immediately before the text in §9.1, below, so there may be something going on here.

gѵedy as dycco y vam yn gyfreithaѵl gysseuyn 'after his mother has first legally affiliated him', *dycco* in the sense of 'affiliated'. The 3 sing. inf. pron. 's is used with the 3 sing. pres. subj. *dycco*, from *dwyn* (*GMW*, §59). On *gysseuyn*, 'first', see above, §5.1, which uses the exact same words: this may be a set legal phrase. This is the only reference to the mother taking part in this process, but she may have affiliated him at birth. The ceremony outlined here, with the head of kindred and the elders formally accepting the son, may be some sort of coming-of-age ceremony within the kindred, making the son a full member.

8.2 penkenedyl ar y seithuet a eill y gymryt 'the head of kindred as one of seven may affiliate him'. See above, §7.9, for *ar y seithuet*.

kymryt o'r penkenedyl dѵylaѵ y mab rѵg y dѵylaѵ ynteu 'the head of kindred takes the two hands of the son between his own two hands', a ceremony of grasping the hands of the child. Both hands are held in the head of kindred's two hands, and this may signify 'possession, custody; authority, power, control' (*GPC*, 'dwylo, dwylaw').

a rodi cussan idaѵ, canys arѵyd kenedyl yѵ cussan 'and gives him a kiss, because the sign of kinship is a kiss'. This refers to ritual kissing, something well known in early Christian societies to 'perform family': the kiss was originally a familial action which was used by early Christian groups, and it was also familiar in early Classical societies (Michael Penn, 'Performing Family: Ritual Kissing and the Construction of Early Christian Kinship', *Journal of Early Christian Studies*, 10.2 (2002), pp. 151-74 (pp. 153-54,

159–61)). Kissing, and passing on kissed elements of the act of worship, was also performed in the medieval church. The priest would kiss the chalice during mass, and then 'transferred the kiss of the chalice […] to the pax', the 'pax' being a tablet marked with a symbol of Christ, and this would be passed around and kissed by the congregation (Orme, *Going to Church*, p. 217). The kiss is a ceremonial and formal action here, along with the hand-holding. The *LlIor* text reads *kerennyd*, an alternative form of *cenedl*, for 'kinship'.

8.3 **y rodi o'r penkenedyl y mab yn llaƀ yr hynaf o'r gƀyr** 'the son is given by the head of kindred into the hand of the eldest of the men'. It is uncertain why the text here reads *y rodi … y mab*, using the poss. pron. *ei*, 'his', and then the n. *y mab*, 'the son'. In *LlIor* the text is different because the son is given by his right hand: *rody llau deheu e mab en llau er hynaf o'r guyr ereyll*, 'the son's right hand is placed in the hand of the eldest of the other men'. This reading makes more sense, and it may be that the change in the wording led to a less coherent construction. The eldest of the men of the kindred, *yr hynaf*, indicates seniority.

ac velly o laƀ y laƀ hyt at y gƀr diƀethaf 'and so from hand to hand until the last of the men'. The child has been given a kiss by the head of kindred, and each of the other six men present take him by his right hand, similar to hand-shaking, to indicate their acceptance of the son into the kindred.

8.4 **Ony byd penkenedyl, vn gƀr ar hugeint o oreugƀyr y genedyl a'e kymer** 'if there is no head of kindred, twenty-one men of the best men in the kindred will affiliate him'. This is the same number of men who deny a son if there is no head of kindred: see above, §7.10.

a chymryt y mab o'r gƀr a vo yn lle yr arglƀyd 'and the son is taken by the man who is in the place of the lord'. This is a detail which is not found in the denial ceremony at §7, above. The use of *yr arglƀyd*, 'the lord', may be a slip, as it would be expected that this would be the head of kindred, although the head of kindred himself would be seen as a lord within his kindred.

erbyn y laƀ deheu idaƀ 'by his right hand', *idaƀ*, 'to him' or 'of his', referring to the son's right hand, and the prep. *erbyn* used in the sense of 'by, by means of'. This is a slight variation to the action performed by the head of kindred himself, perhaps because this is someone standing in for him; rather than taking both the son's hands between his hands, this time the acting head of kindred takes the son by the right hand, kisses him, and then he is passed along the line, *o laƀ y laƀ*, 'from hand to hand'.

hyt at y gƀr diƀethaf o hynny o ƀyr 'until the last man of those men'. Once he has touched the hand of the last of the selected twenty-one men from the kindred, he has been formally accepted into the kindred and is a full member with all the rights.

§9

9.1 **O deruyd geni dyn** 'if it happens that a man is born'. The use of *dyn*, 'a man', is unusual, and in general *mab*, 'son', or *merch*, 'daughter', is used, but the subject matter of this *damwain* is concerned with the gender of the child and it may be that *dyn* is used here to refer to 'a human' irrespective of gender.

ac aelodeu gѵr ac vn gѵreic idaѵ 'and they have male members and a female one': my suggested translations for this section will use gender neutral pronouns, e.g. 'they', unless the text explicitly refers to masculine or feminine. *Aelodau* generally refers to male genitalia, those of a *gwr*, 'man' (*GPC*, 'aelod'), and it is clearly linked to *gwr* in this sentence. The child is intersex because they have visible male reproductive parts *ac vn gѵreic*, 'and that of a woman', *gwraig* referring to a grown woman rather than a girl (see §1.1), and *vn*, 'one, that one', referring to the visible female reproductive part — sing., *un*. The 3 sing. m. prep. *i*, 'to', is used, but MW does not have a neuter corresponding to English 'it'.

Later dictionaries have *gwrwraig* as the word for an intersex person, and the word was used by Dafydd ap Gwilym (*GPC*, 'gwrwraig'; the terminology and its development is discussed more fully in Luke Blaidd's forthcoming study), but *gwrwraig* was not used in this text, perhaps because the writers preferred to use distinct words as the legal status is the important element in this section. However, *gwrwraig* is used in the heading for this section in K (NLW, Peniarth MS 40, p. 216), in red and in the margin; this manuscript is in the hand of the poet and scribe Lewys Glyn Cothi, who was clearly aware of the word and what it meant.

ac yn petrus py ardelu a vo gantaѵ 'and it is uncertain what legal status they have'. The word *arddelw* is well known in the laws, and is a legal stance taken by the parties in a legal case: it can be translated as 'case', 'plea', 'warranty' (*LTMW*, p. 313). The word itself derives from *delw*, 'image, form', but *GPC* notes that some of the examples listed under the first sense may belong to the second, meaning 'to acknowledge, avow, own, profess […] hold' (*LTMW*, p. 313; *GPC*, 'arddel¹, arddelw¹', 'arddelaf, arddelwaf: arddel², arddelw², arddelwi, arddelu'). Wiliam suggests the translation 'character, role, legal personality' for *arddelw* (*LlIor*, p. 144), and in his note on a particular example he states that *arddelw* means '"rôle, part, character": the rôle assumed in law, the legal personage', which a person would have to choose if there were options (*LlIor*, p. 113). The meaning is clearly similar here, where it means the identity which the child has, or the form of their legal status. *Petrus* means 'uncertain', and *py* is the interr. pron., *pa* in ModW (and also further on in this sentence), meaning 'which'. Because there are no neuter forms in MW, m. forms and mutations are used by the creators of this section, but that does not mean that they are assigning a gender to the person.

rei a dyḃeit 'some say'. See §2.4, above.

dylyu etrych o pa aruer yd aruero 'it should be looked to see which practice they practise', *aruer* as a noun referring to 'practice' or 'use', i.e. the type of *arddelw*, 'legal role', they use. *Dylyu etrych* is the v.n., and *etrych* is *edrych*, 'to look'. *Yd aruero* is the 3 sing. pres. subj. of *arfer*.

a herḃyd yd aruero kerdet y vreint 'and according to the way they practice is the value of their status', 'according to their practice goes the value of their status'. *Herwydd* is commonly used as a conj. in the laws, meaning 'according to' (*GMW*, §268), so this states 'according to the way they practice', with the determination of their status at the end of the sentence. *Kerdet* is used here in a legal sense — not *cerdded*, 'to walk' — which Wiliam notes in his index and glossary can mean 'status' (*LlIor*, p. 147), but perhaps 'value' or 'price' is more accurate, and *GPC* notes this sense for the noun (*GPC*, 'cerddaf', as a n., b). It is used for valuing animals in the laws, e.g. *Dynawet guryu un gerdet yu a dynawet uanyu*, 'a male yearling is of the same value as a female yearling' (*LlIor*, §128/1; Jenkins translates it as 'same progress', *LTMW*, p. 176, l. 19); *canys hanner kerdet gauyr yu er eydy*, 'for her value is half that of a goat' (*LlIor*, §130/6; *LTMW*, p. 180, l. 11); *ac urth henne e mae un gerdet hy a llo buuch*, 'and therefore it is of the same value as a cow's calf' (*LlIor*, §138/8). Jenkins again has 'same progress' in his translation (*LTMW*, p. 188, l. 34), but see also Rodway and Williams who note that 'We have emended Jenkins's translation of *kerdet* from "progress" to "value"' (Simon Rodway and Myriah Williams, 'Bullo .i. bronnced?: Another Look at Two Obscure Words for Horse Tack in *De raris fabulis*', *CMCS*, 83 (2022), pp. 49–63 (p. 57, n. 47)).

9.2 **Os o pob vn yd aruerha ef, kyfreith a dyḃeit dylyu kerdet y vreint ḃrth y breint ychaf** 'if they practice all of them, the law says that their status is valued at the highest status', and the higher status is as a man. The law lets the individual choose their gender identity. They are not forced to choose in a final sense, and may identify as both male and female: *pob vn*, 'all of them', usually refers to all of several. However, if they do not choose to identify as female, they will automatically be assigned male status as it is higher in value. Traditionally gender was conferred at baptism, and the baby would be given a masculine or feminine name (Orme, *Medieval Children*, p. 328), but this may not have been possible in this case. See also §2.5, above.

sef yḃ hḃnnḃ, breint gḃr, a dylyu tref tat ohonaḃ 'that is, the status of a man, and they are entitled to patrimony'. See §7.14. The latter part of this sentence is ambiguous; if the *a* is a conj. 'and', then the sentence divides into clauses: the demonstrative *sef yḃ hḃnnḃ* with the answer *breint gḃr*, and then the additional information that if he is classified as a man, he would then be entitled to receive land.

9.3 **Ac o beichogir ef, caffel o'e vab tref y tat o vreint y gŵr a'e beichoges** 'and if they become pregnant, their son receives patrimony according to the status of the man who made them pregnant'. On *beichogir* and *beichoges* see §2.1; *caffael*, §1.7, §6.1; *tref y tat*, §7.14; and *vreint*, §2.6. At this point male pronouns are being used: the person has become pregnant. It is not clear how they identify, but the lawyers' focus is on a son born to the person, who would be entitled to land: they would have the status of the man who made the intersex person pregnant.

or beichocca ynteu ŵreic arall, caffel o'e vab ef tref y tat 'if he impregnates another woman, his son receives his patrimony', using the m. pron. for the person causing the pregnancy, but in fact keeping the options open, because *wraig arall*, 'another woman', could refer to someone who is identifying as a woman impregnating another woman. M. pronouns are used for the rule regarding the son born from a woman and the person as they were acting in a male capacity according to the law. The child of this union would receive their inheritance through the intersex person, since they had impregnated the mother.

9.4 *LlIor* has a version of this *damwain*, with similar wording (although not using the *damwain* opening, *O derfydd*) following Land Law, in a section discussing royal rights to land (*LlIor*, §94/10; *LTMW*, p. 126, ll. 9–12). Anderson notes that the example in Land Law is the only reference to fosterage in the Welsh laws, but it is also clearly referred to in this *damwain* (Anderson, '*Urth noe e tat*', p. 3).

vab vchelŵr 'noble', although despite the use of *fab*, 'son', it simply means 'male noble', and *uchelwr* and *mab uchelwr* are both used interchangeably. Here, the *mab uchelwr* is giving his *mab*, his 'son', to another to rear. Other words for this rank in society are used in the laws, where we see *bonheddig* (*canhwynol*), 'innate nobleman', and *breyr*, 'nobleman': see notes on *bonheddig canhwynol*, §3.12. *Uchelwr*, *uchel* + *gŵr*, 'high + man', is a synonym for *breyr* and in Latin is *optimas* or *nobilis*, meaning a 'nobleman' (*LTMW*, p. 389).

rodi y vab ar veithrin 'place his son on fosterage'. *Meithrin* is the word for 'rear, bring up', but it also refers to fosterage, sending a son to another family — not his birth parents — who would rear him until he reached a certain age: 'the usual form of artificial kinship (kinship created by a deliberate act where none existed before) in both Ireland and Wales was fosterage' (Charles-Edwards, *Kinship*, p. 78). This is perhaps better known in the context of Ireland, but this section supports Anderson's conclusion that it was being practised in Wales too, but as a 'distinctive and much more limited kind of fosterage' (Anderson, '*Urth Noe e Tat*', pp. 10–11).

at daya𝛖c o ganyat y argl𝛖yd 'to a bondsman with the permission of his lord'. On *taeog*, 'bondsman', see §1.1. In the bond society, the bondsmen were owned to some extent by their lords, and it is the bondsman's lord who would need to give the bondsman permission to take on the rearing of the child through fosterage. *LlIor* has *ar uab eyllt argluyd*, 'with the *aillt* of the lord', *aillt* being one of the three words for 'unfree persons' (*LlIor*, §94/10; *LTMW*, p. 126, and p. 310). It appears that fosterage in Wales was limited to the upper levels of society (Anderson, 'Urth Noe e Tat', p. 9).

a'e uagu o'r taya𝛖c vl𝛖ydyn ae d𝛖y ae teir 'and he is reared by the bondsman for a year or two or three'. This takes us beyond the early years, and the description found earlier in this text — in the Blegywryd texts — of rearing a noble son, which focuses on breastfeeding, see §1, above. Smith notes that fosterage 'might well commence only after the wet-nursing period had terminated', and clearly it carried on for much longer, perhaps for the remainder of his childhood, and involved 'the upbringing, training and education of the child long after the immediate physical needs of early infancy had been fulfilled' (Smith, 'Fosterage, Adoption, and God-parenthood', p. 13).

ony byd plant ida𝛖, y dylyet oll a dyg𝛖yd yn lla𝛖 y mab maeth 'unless he has children, all of his inheritance will pass into the hand of the foster son'. The Welsh laws do not discuss adoption — perhaps because it was not necessary; children could be affiliated to a father or made part of a kindred following a different process, as is seen in this text. But this section states that the foster child would inherit all of his bond father's inheritance if his foster-father had no other children (Smith, 'Fosterage, Adoption, and God-parenthood', pp. 18–19). *Dylyet*, the noun from the same root as the vb *dyly*, means 'to be entitled', and here it refers to inheritance of land; see §1.2. *Dyg𝛖yd* is not the vb from *dwyn*, 'to take, to lead', but from *digwydd*, 'to befall', with the meaning 'to pass into the possession of, fall into the hands of', here with the addition of *yn llaw*, 'into the hands' (*GPC*, 'digwyddaf'). See also §7.12.

9.5   **kymeint a phop vn o'e ueibon a geiff y mab maeth** 'the foster son will receive as much as every one of his sons'. This refers to *cyfran*, used in Welsh law, where all of the sons would receive a share of their father's land on his death. It is the opposite of primogeniture, where the firstborn son receives all of the land, common in England in the same period. The rules on dividing land between brothers are detailed in *LlIor*, and this is the preoccupation behind the entire system of affiliation into a kindred and denial from a kindred, discussed here: the son would be another man who would receive a share of the father's land (*LlIor*, §82; *LTMW*, pp. 98–100). It is clear that the son, in this section of text, has rights equal to his foster-brothers (Smith, 'Fosterage, Adoption, and God-parenthood', pp. 18–19), and it is not simply a case of being the sole heir of a childless man. This would not be a positive outcome for the bondsman, and perhaps this is why it was described in that way in a triad: *Teir pla kenedyl: magu mab arglvyd, a dvyn mab y genedyl yg kam, a guarchadv penreith*, 'The three plagues of a kindred: rearing a lord's son, and affiliating a child wrongly to a kindred, and guarding the chief compurgator' (*LT*, W82). It is striking that another of the plagues in the triad also refers to affiliating children. Fosterage may have been intended in some circumstances to break down the barriers between the social classes, and give children of *uchelwyr* experience of dealing with the lower classes (Smith, 'Fosterage, Adoption, and God-parenthood', p. 25).

9.6 The following two *damweiniau*, the first on twins, and the second on denying a daughter from a kindred, occur together in most of the *damweiniau* collections, although they are not closely connected in subject.

geni deu uab yn vn torllẃyth 'two sons are born from one pregnancy', in other words, twin boys. The word *torllwyth*, 'litter', is generally used of animals rather than humans in the modern usage, but as the word means 'belly load', it can refer to people as well as animals, so it means 'human pregnancy' here.

a'r torllẃyth yn ieuaf o blant y tat 'and this pregnancy is the youngest of the father's children', with *torllwyth* again being used for multiple birth. These twin boys have older siblings, and they are the youngest of the father's children.

iaẃn yẃ y'r vam gẃybot pẃy diẃethaf a anet ohonunt 'it is right for the mother to know which of them was the last to be born', with the pl. prep. *ohonunt*, 'of them', at the end of the clause. The order of birth is important, and since one of the boys will be the youngest of the father's sons, the mother must be certain which was born first and which was born second.

ẃrth gaffel y tydyn kyfreithaẃl ohonaẃ 'because he gets the legal homestead/dwelling-place'. Jenkins notes that 'etymologically *tyddyn* implies a plot of land carrying a house (*tŷ*), and "homestead" is used as a rough equivalent, though some passages suggest that the *tyddyn* did not necessarily have buildings on it; perhaps the essential feature of the *tyddyn* was that the land was enclosed' (*LTMW*, p. 386; see also *GPC*, 'tyddyn'). In the section called 'Sharing of Land' in Jenkins's translation, it gives instructions on how brothers are to share land between them: the youngest son has an important role in 'dividing the whole patrimony' if there are no houses on the land, but if there are houses, the second-youngest divides and the youngest chooses first (*LTMW*, p. 99, ll. 13–21). Cyfnerth and Blegywryd have similar rules, and the youngest brother gets a specified share, the *tyddyn arbennig*, 'special homestead' — 'the special croft and eight acres, and all the buildings' (*LTMW*, p. 99, ll. 22–30). It is

9.7 **Ac yna y byd geir geir y mam y rydunt** 'and then the mother's word will be final between them'. The phrase *gair ei gair* (f.) or *gair ei air* (m.), here without a poss. pron., occurs in the laws, and the word *gair*, 'word', has two functions. In this example the first *gair* means 'decision, dictum, decree; testimony', in the sense of 'final word' to settle the matter (*GPC*, 'gair⁴'). The second *gair* is in the basic sense of 'word', and it refers to the means of making the decision — the mother's word is all that is required to settle the case between them with no requirement to swear a formal oath.

Y rydunt is the prep. *rhwng*, 'between', and the variant form with a *y*, *y rhwng*, is not uncommon in MW (*GMW*, §236 '(Y)rwng'; *GPC*, 'rhwng, yrhwng'); it is the form used in this particular section of text — see §9.8, below.

9.8 **Or deruyd na ƀypper pƀy diƀethaf pƀy gyntaf** 'If it happens that it is not known who is last and who is first', with *gwybod* in the imps. pres. subj. Either the mother does not know, or she may have died in childbirth. There is no suggestion that there would be a midwife or another woman present at the birth who could give testimony instead of the mother, and there is no procedure for doing so.

diheu yƀ bot y neill o'r torllƀyth hƀnnƀ yn ol 'it is certain that one of them is after'. The adj. *y neill* by itself, without *llall, arall* means 'one (of two)' (*GMW*, §96). The reading *yn ol*, 'after' or 'behind', meaning 'last', is not found in other versions of this text: D has *diheu yƀ bot y torllƀyth hƀnnƀ yn diwethaf*, 'it is certain that that pregnancy is the last'; F has *diheu yƀ hagen bot y torllƀyth hƀnnƀ yn ieuhaf y neill onadunt*, 'it is certain however that of that pregnancy one of them is the youngest'; Col has *ac en dyheu bot e torlluyd hunnu en yeuaf ac o hunnu e neyll en yeu no'r llall*, 'and it is certain that that pregnancy is the youngest and from that one of them is younger than the other'; and K has *dieu yƀ bot y naill o'r torllƀyth hƀnnƀ*, 'it is certain that it is one from that pregnancy' (i.e. is the youngest). The text is attempting to express that one of the twin boys must be the youngest or the last, with Q stating one of them is *yn ol*, 'after [the other]'. One of them has to be younger than the other, but as it is impossible to decide which, the law suggests an alternative.

a hƀnnƀ a renir yn deu hanner y rydunt 'and that is divided in two halves between them'. The land or the 'homestead' which is due to the youngest son is divided between the two of them since it cannot be determined which is actually the youngest son. *Y rydunt* is the 3 pl. of the prep. *rhwng*, 'between' (see §9.7, above).

canys kyhyded yƀ y rydunt 'because it is equality between them', 'because they have an equal claim between them'. *Cyhydedd* is literally 'of equal length', *cy* + *hyd*, 'length', but it is used in the laws to mean an equal share, 'equality of entitlement', or simply 'equality'; *kydyded yv*, 'it is equal/ equality'. There are some references in the lawbooks to *cyfraith cyhydedd*, 'the law of equality', particularly in Land Law (e.g. *LlIor*, §80/3, *LTMW*, p. 95, l. 6; *LlIor*, §85/4, *LTMW*, p. 104, l. 24): Jenkins notes that 'Practical concern for justice is most clearly seen in the application of *cyfraith gyhydedd*, "the law of equality", according to which the subject-matter of a dispute could be equally shared between the parties' (*LTMW*, p. xxxv). Col refers to *cyfraith cyhydedd* in its version of this text: the homestead is to be divided in half *herwyd keureyth cehedet*, 'according to the law of equality'.

9.9 **Ereill o'r ygneit a dyveit** 'others of the lawyers say', or 'others among the lawyers say'. Only Q and K have the reference to lawyers; D, F, and Col simply have *ereill a dyweit*, 'others say', not specifying that these are lawyers. On the other opinions, see §2.1.

yny vyppo yn diheu y vot ef yn vab ieuaf, na dyly ef breint y mab ieuaf 'until it is known for certain that he is the youngest son, he is not entitled to the inheritance of the youngest son'. On *yny* and doubt see §5.1. *Breint*, 'privilege', is used here for the inheritance, or special status in relation to the land, the youngest son's share. The text is the same in Q and D, but F has *na dyly ynteu tydyn y mab ieuaf*, 'he is not entitled to the youngest son's homestead' (with the term *tydyn arbenhic*, 'special homestead' in the same passage); K has *rann y map ieuaf*, 'the youngest son's share'; and Col has *tedyn y tat*, 'the father's homestead'. The other lawyers disagree with dividing the homestead: a man is not entitled to the special share reserved to the youngest son if it is not certain that he is the youngest son. These other lawyers do not suggest a solution to the problem, but it seems that the other view is that dividing the land between them should not apply in this case.

9.10 Following the *damwain* on twins, this one — which usually appears immediately after the one on twins — discusses denial of a daughter, and is on a similar theme to the discussion in §7.12–15, on possible abuses of the affiliation or denial process.

Or deruyd gvadu merch o genedyl, a'e rodi y vr 'If it happens that a girl is denied by a kindred, and she is given to a husband' (on *o genedyl*, the agent of the denial, see *GMW*, §181(a)). In general the laws do not discuss denial or acceptance of daughters, since they do not have a role in land inheritance. However, this *damwain* discusses a situation where there would be a financial implication for the kindred or father's family — the amobr payment to the lord when the girl is married.

a bot amrysson am y hamobyr 'and there is dispute over her amobr', in that the kindred are perhaps trying to avoid paying the amobr payment to the lord because the girl has been denied before marriage. On *amobr* see §4.4.

kyfreith a dyḇeit pan yḇ yr arglḇyd a'e dyly, canyt oes perchennaḇc a'e dylyo 'the law says that it is the lord who is entitled to it, since there is no other owner who is entitled to it'. On *pan yw* see §2.2. This is a problematic section of text, and there are different versions in the manuscripts: D simply says that the lord is entitled to the amobr but does not have the part which says that there is no owner (*AL*, V.ii.59). Col has *canyt oes perchennauc arall a'y deleho*, 'because there is no other owner who is entitled to it' (*DwC*, 314). This reference to the *perchennog*, 'owner', may be an attempt to link this to *diffaith brenin*, 'the king's waste', see below. The amobr, or indeed the girl, has no 'owner' as the girl has been denied by her kindred and is therefore without a father or kindred to pay amobr. *Dylyo* — see §1.2, and the discussion on the use of the word in the laws — could also mean that there is no owner who 'owes it'. The statement is strange since the amobr payment always goes to the lord, and nobody else would have a right to it.

a hḇnnḇ yn diffeith brenhin y byd 'and that one will be the king's waste'. The syntax is unusual here with *y byd*, from *bod*, 'will be', at the end of the sentence: it is unnecessary and is only found in Q. The reference to *diffaith brenin*, 'the king's waste', is not found in K. *Diffaith brenin* is defined as goods without an owner: *Pob da hep perchennavc ydau esyd dyffeyth brenhyn*, 'All goods without an owner are King's waste' (*Lllor*, §43/7, *LTMW*, p. 41, l. 16). The concept does not quite work in this scenario: *diffaith brenin* are ownerless goods which go to the lord, as a bonus; but here he is owed amobr but there is nobody to pay it, so he presumably does not receive anything. It may be that *diffaith* is used in the sense of barren, desolate, as a loss to the lord, a payment which is written off.

9.11 **Os Kymraes vyd y mam, kymeint vyd y hamobyr ac vn bonhedic kanhḇynaḇl, nyt amgen, pedeir ar hugeint** 'If the mother is a Welsh woman, her amobr will be as much as that for an innate noblewoman, namely, twenty-four'. On *Cymraes* see §6.7, above. A Welsh woman's amobr — in this case — is calculated as if she were the daughter of an 'innate nobleman', see §3.12. The text in Q states that this is *pedair ar hugeint*, 'twenty-four', but this is not correct according to the list of amobr prices in the law, where twenty-four pence is the sum for an alien's daughter (see *Lllor*, §51/13, *LTMW*, p. 55, ll. 3–9). In *Lllor*, the amount for an *aillt*'s, 'nobleman's', daughter is given as *try ugeynt*, 'three score', although some manuscripts read *pedwar ugeint*, 'four score' (*Lllor*, §51/13, and variant 5). In this *damwain*, D, F, and Col read *pedwar ugeint*, 'four score' (*AL*, V.ii.59; *DwC*, 314), but Q, J, and K have *pedair ar hugain*, 'twenty-four' (*pedair* as f. presumably because it refers to pence); this is no doubt an error for *pedwar ugain*. J does not have a sum but states that *kymaint vyd amobyr y verch a'r uam*, 'the daughter's amobr will be as much as her mother's' (*J(ed.)*, p. 129, l. 5).

9.12 **Os alltudes vyd y mam kymeint vyd a'e mam ac vn merch alltut** 'If the mother is an alien it will be as much as her mother's and that of an alien's daughter'. The text may have been amended here, but it is an attempt to say that if the mother is an alien, the daughter's amobr will be the same as her mother's would be, and that is the same as the amobr of an alien's daughter. In the laws, this is calculated at twenty-four pence (*LlIor*, §51/13, *LTMW*, p. 55, ll. 3–9).

9.13 **Ac velly vyd ebediỽ mab a ỽatter** 'And in the same way the *ebediw* of a son who is denied'. *Ebediw* is the death duty, and it is calculated according to status: see §3.4. *Ebediw* and amobr are often linked in the laws, and the price of a woman's amobr is the same as her husband or father's *ebediw*. Here, the same method is used for calculating the *ebediw* of a denied son: he is priced as an innate nobleman, or an alien.

ony byd kynydu ohonaỽ o vreint mal y dyrchauo ar y ebediỽ 'unless his status increases so that his *ebediw* is raised'. *Dyrchauo ar y ebediỽ*, literally 'he increases on his *ebediw*', i.e. his *ebediw* increases, *dyrchafu* meaning 'to increase'. This would happen if there was a change to his status in some way — by getting an office, or by a change in his status in relation to land.

9.14 This is a short explanation, presented as a *damwain*, of the definition of a *mab dioddef*, 'a son by sufferance': see also §7.1.

Or deruyd tebygu 'If it happens that it is thought'. This shows legal discussion or thought, as with the phrase *rei a dyweit*, 'some say', §2.1. Here it refers to assumptions made about the laws, rather than to other legal authorities; when this phrase occurs, it is usually wrong, and the correct answer according to the law follows.

bot yn uab diodef pop mab diodef a dyỽetter y uot yn vab dyn 'that every son by sufferance who is said to be a man's son is a son by sufferance'. A complicated sentence with the repeat of *mab diodef*, 'son by sufferance', see §7.1. The discussion is about a man's purported son when the father has suffered him (without acceptance or denial): the question is whether that son fits the legal definition of a 'son by sufferance'. The child called *mab dioddef* is one the father is putting up with, and *a dywetter*, 'it is said' — imps. pres. subj. of *dweud*, 'to say, to state' — *y uot yn vab dyn*, 'that he is the son of a man'. The child has been linked to the father by word of mouth, and has been suffered by the so-called father who has not started any legal process to accept or deny him. The answer to the question follows.

y gyfreith a dyỽeit nat mab diodef 'the law says that he is not a son by sufferance'. The answer is that he does not fit the legal definition of *mab dioddef*. The reading in Q and K is *hyt nat mab diodef*, but the exact

9.15 **mab a dycco y uam yn gyfreithaẞl kyny chymerer, ny ẞatẞyt** 'a son which the mother affiliates lawfully although he is not accepted, he has not been denied'. *Cymerer* and *gwadwyd* are in different tenses, and *gwadwyd* constitutes a new main clause. This gives a definition of a *mab dioddef*. The mother has made the formal statement naming the father of her son, but the father (or kindred) have not answered one way or another; the son is linked to a father but is not formally accepted. Because of this, he is not a denied son. However, the point seems to be that in this case given here, the mother has not made her legal statement: it is only hearsay that links the son to the man, and so he is not a *mab dioddef* in the specific legal sense.

ac ẞrth na ẞadẞyt, diodeuedic yẞ 'and because he has not been denied, he is suffered'. A son who has been accepted by his father is his son; if he is denied by the father, he is not his son. This son is in-between: he has been presented by the mother, but has not been denied or accepted, although the father is putting up with him. He is *dioddefedig*, a vbl adj. meaning 'suffered', or 'under sufferance'.

a hẞnnẞ ny ellir y ẞadu rac y gyfulauan 'and that one cannot be denied because of his offence': he cannot be denied as a reaction to a serious offence or killing (*cyflafan*, see §6.6) he has committed. The version in Q may be missing a bit: Col adds *eny dywyco*, 'unless it is compensated', at the end of the sentence, and K similarly has *yni diẞyco y gyulauan*, 'unless the offence is compensated' (*DwC*, 319; *AL*, VI.i.4). If the son is to be denied from the kindred, all compensation for his actions must be paid first.

J has a different version which explains the situation in a different way: *a hwnnw ny dylyir gwadu y gyflafan a wnel, cany wadwyt ef pan y duc y vam*, 'and the offence that that one commits is not to be denied, because he was not denied when the mother affiliated him' (*J(ed.)*, p. 129, ll. 17–18).

9.16 This *damwain* discusses the situation with the son of a mute woman, and the procedure to deny or affiliate him. It emphasizes the mother's role in the process, and the limits on the mother in this case because of her disability.

ẞreic vut 'mute woman'. Mute people had fewer rights in Welsh law, because of the emphasis on speaking to state legal cases (see *LT*, p. 260, and p. 263 where a man with a speech impediment is not permitted to speak in court or is not able to do so). It is stated in one place that a mute man may not inherit land (see the discussion in Pryce, *Native Law and the Church*, p. 105). These punishing rules are linked with the importance placed in the laws on being able to argue the case using words and speech.

a'e ammeu o genedyl y tat 'and he is doubted by the father's kindred', *ammeu*, or *amau*, meaning 'to suspect' or 'to doubt': the father's family suspect that the son is not theirs.

nyt reit y genedyl y tat na'e ɓadu na'e gymryt, onys mynnant 'the father's kindred do not have to deny him or accept him, unless they wish it'. The formal legal process does not have to be followed here — it seems that the kindred decide on the child's membership of the kindred without having to follow any legal process. They may do so if they wish: *onys* is the conj. *oni*, 'unless', with the 3 sing. inf. pron. *'s*, 'it', and *mynnant* is the 3 pl. pres. ind. of *mynnu*, 'to want, to wish'.

kany dyɓeit ehun y dyuot yn eidunt ɓy 'because she herself does not state that he is theirs'. The person is unclear in *kany dyɓeit ehun*, 'since he himself/she herself does not state', but other readings show that this text is discussing the mother. Col and D have *hi*, 'she'; F has *y vam*, 'the mother'; there is eye-skip in J at this point (*DwC*, 268; *AL*, V.ii.35 and variant 3; *J(ed.)*, p. 128, ll. 26). Q and K share the same reading. This is the mother, and she has not said (out loud) that the son belongs to them; she cannot do so because she is mute. *Eidunt hwy*, 'belongs to them', is from the noun *eiddo*, 'belonging [to]', and with the predicative part. *yn* it means 'as theirs, as their belonging'; it also takes a plural ending *-unt* (*GPC*, 'eiddo¹' c; and *GMW*, §57).

9.17 **Gɓedy bo marɓ** 'after she is dead'. Again in Q it is not clear who has died, but Q's sister-text for the *damweiniau*, K, has *gɓedi bo uarɓ y uam*, 'after his/the mother has died', and all of the other versions also have *y fam* to make it clear that the mother has died. The point is that in Welsh law, the mother initiates the affiliation process, and if the mother is living but has not started the process, it must wait until she has died. This is irrespective of her disability.

ef a digaɓn ymyrru ar y genedl 'he is able to take action on the kindred'. *Ef a digawn* means 'he is able to' (*GPC*, 'digonaf' b; and see §7.12). *Ymyrru* is difficult and has several meanings: it can mean to interfere or intervene, and Jenkins suggests that it is used in this way in the laws (*LTMW*, p. 393, two examples). It is often neg., with a sense of unwanted interference, but it has a further meaning of 'take part, act' (*GPC*, 'ymyrraf'). The context makes it clear that the son in this passage is able to initiate the legal process once his mother has died, and it may be that this is a reflexive form of *gyrru*, in the legal sense of 'to accuse, charge with, prosecute, carry on a lawsuit' (*GPC*, 'gyrru⁷'), although *ymyrru* is not attested in this way in any other text. The word *ymyrru* is found in all versions of this text.

ony ɓedir yn gyfreithaɓl a'e uot yn gymeredic 'unless he is denied lawfully and he has been affiliated'. Only Q and K share this reading, and it may be a defective text: the other versions state that the next step is to deny or affiliate him: *a gwedy hynny reit uyd ae gymryt ae wadu*, 'and after that he must be either affiliated or denied' (*J(ed.)*, p. 128, ll. 28–29). Q and K use the imps. pres. ind. *wedir*, 'deny', to say that he may be denied or be affiliated, although the conj. *a'e* in the clause *a'e uot yn gymeredic*, 'and he has been affiliated', states that he is already affiliated.

GLOSSARY

The glossary is arranged according to the Welsh alphabet, with the Middle Welsh graphs listed under their modern equivalent, e.g. k as c, v as f or u, and ỽ as w (this particular manuscript is consistent in its use of ỽ and does not use the form <w>). Items are listed under their radical initial consonant, although lenited forms which may be confusing have been listed in the form in which they appear, with a cross reference to the radical form. Conjugated verb forms are listed under the verb noun, and forms which may cause confusion are listed in the glossary with cross references to the verb noun. Where the verb noun is not given in the text, it is listed in the glossary in ModW, in brackets after the conjugated form(s) and the text references. Almost all words which occur in the text are listed here. In cases where there are numerous instances of a word or form, the first three examples are given. Where words are spelled in an unusual way, the more common or ModW spelling is given in inverted commas and in brackets. References are to section numbers followed by sentence number, e.g. 1.1, and cases where there is a note explaining a particular form or the meaning of a technical legal term are indicated by an 'n' attached to the reference. See also the list of Grammatical Abbreviations at the start of this volume.

A

a¹, ac (usually before vowels) conj. *and* 1.1, 1.3, 1.4; with def. art. **a'r** 5.3, 6.4, 9.6; with 3 sing. f. inf. poss. pron. **a'e** 1.4, 1.6, 7.14; with 3 pl. inf. poss. pron. **a'e** 7.15
a² rel. pron. *who, which, that* 1.1, 1.2, 1.4; with 3 sing. m. inf. obj. pron. **a'e** 1.2, 1.3; with 3 pl. inf. obj. pron. **a'e** 1.7
a³ prep. introducing comparison, *as, that* 3.2, 3.12, 6.9; **a'e** with 3 sing. f. inf. obj. pron. 9.12
a⁴, ac (before vowels) prep. *with* 6.8, 7.14
a⁵ pvbl part. 1.1, 1.2, 1.4
a⁶ see **mynet**
achaỽs, achos n. *cause, reason* 6.6; **sef achos** with dem. [*this is*] *because*, [*this is*] *why, the reason is* 2.3, 6.2
a dan compound prep. *under* 2.10
adỽna 3 sing. pres. ind. *to undo* 6.3 (v.n. **adwneud, adwneuthur**)
ae part. *either* 2.1, 2.4, 5.7, 9.1, 9.4
aelodeu n. pl. *parts, members* [*of body*] 2.3, 9.1
allan adv. [*from then*] *onwards* 2.10, 3.9, 3.11

allaỽr n. *altar* 5.3, 5.8
alltudes n. *female alien, foreign woman* 7.5, 9.12
alltut n. *alien, foreigner* 5.5, 6.7, 7.5
am prep. *around, for, about* 2.1, 2.8, 3.8, 5.9, 9.10; **amdanaỽ** 3 sing. m. prep. *for it* 2.1, 2.2
amgen, nyt amgen phrase *namely* 9.11, 9.12
ammeu v.n. *doubt* 9.16
amobyr n. *virginity payment, payable to a lord on a girl's marriage* 4.4n, 9.10, 9.11
amrysson n. *dispute, debate* 9.10
amser n. *time* 3.2
annodeu n. *inadvertence* 2.8n
annolo, anolo adj. *useless* 5.1n
ar¹ prep. *on* 1.1, 1.5, 2.6; **arnei** 3 sing. f. *on her* 4.3, 4.4, 4.6, 5.3, 5.8; **arnaỽ** 3 sing. m. *on him/it* 2.3, 2.5, 2.10, 3.1, 3.2, 6.4; **ar** with num. and n. *fourteen*, 3.1, 3.4, 3.6, 3.11, 4.6; *twenty-one* 7.10, 8.4; *twenty-four* 9.11, 9.12
ar² dem. pron. 3.8
ar y seithvet see **seithuet**
arall¹ adj. *other, another* 6.2, 6.6, 9.3
arall² pron. *other, another [person]* 1.7, 6.6
ardelu n. *identity, legal status* 9.1n
aruer n. *practice* 9.1
aruerha 3 sing. pres. ind. *practise* 9.2; **aruero** 3 sing. pres. subj. 9.1 (v.n. **arfer**)
arglỽyd n. *lord* 3.1, 3.6, 3.7, 3.11, 8.4, 9.4, 9.10
arỽyd n. *sign* 8.2
as see **gỽedy as**
asseu adj. *left* 5.3, 5.8
at prep. *to, towards* 3.6, 8.3, 8.4, 9.4
atteb¹ n. *answer, response* 3.2
atteb² v.n. *to answer* 5.1

B

bara n. *bread* 5.6
barnu v.n. *to judge* 2.5
bedyd n. *baptism* 5.3
bedydyer imps. pres. subj. *baptize* 2.5n, 2.6, 4.1 (v.n. **bedyddio**)
beichogi n. *foetus, pregnancy* 2.1, 4.6
beichogi v.n. *to become pregnant, to impregnate* 2.6; **beichocca** 3 sing. pres. ind. 9.3; **beichoges** 3 sing. pret. 9.3; **beichogir** imps. pres. ind. 9.3
bieu vbl phrase (**pieu** + pron.) *to belong to, the duty of* 2.10n, 6.6
blaen n. *front* 5.3, 5.8
blith adj. *milch* 1.6

blodeua 3 sing. pres. ind. *flowers (lit.), menstruates* 4.3 (v.n. **blodeuo**)

blŵydyn n. *year* 1.3, 7.3; **blŵyd** n. *a year* 2.7, 3.1, 3.4, 3.11, 4.2; **blyned** (following numbers) 2.10, 3.6, 4.1

bonhedic adj. or substantive n. *noble* 1.2; **bonhedic canhŵynaŵl** *innate nobleman* 3.12n, 6.9, 7.6, 9.11

bot v.n. *to be* 2.5, 3.1, 3.2; **bei** 3 sing. impf. subj. 6.6, 7.9; **bo** 3 sing. pres. subj. 3.1, 3.4, 3.11; **boet** 3 sing. pres. subj. 7.5; **bu** 3 sing. pret. 6.6; **byd** 3 sing. pres. habit./fut. ind. 2.3, 2.6, 2.10; **y mae** 3 sing. pres. ind. 3.7, 5.2; **maent** 3 pl. pres. ind. 7.13; **ynt** 3 pl. pres. ind. 6.9; **yssyd** 3 sing. pres. ind. 2.1, 5.3, 5.8, 7.13; **yŵ** 3 sing. pres. ind. 2.2, 2.3, 2.4

braŵt n. *brother* 7.12, 7.14, 7.15

breint n. *status* 2.6n, 3.7, 3.12; **ymreint** (with prep. **yn²**) 3.3n, 3.5, 3.12

brenhin n. *king* 2.7, 2.8, 7.5, 9.1; see also **diffeith brenin**

brethyn n. *cloth [wool]* 1.5

brith adj. *speckled, coloured* 1.5

bronneu n. pl. *breasts* 4.3

buch n. *cow* 1.1, 1.6

bŵyll see **pŵyll**

bynnac: **pŵy bynnac** grammaticalized phrase *whoever* 5.1; **pa … bynnag** grammaticalized phrase *whichever* 5.2

byth adv. *always, forever* 6.1, 6.2, 6.3, 7.3

byŵ adj. *alive* 3.4, 7.9

C/K

kaffel v.n. *to have* 6.1n, 9.3, 9.6; **caffo** 3 sing. pres. subj. 4.4; **keiff** 3 sing. pres. ind. 1.1, 1.7, 9.5

calhon n. *heart* 5.3n, 5.8

camlŵrŵ n. *fine* (3 cows or 180 pence) 2.7n

canhŵynaŵl, see **bonhedic canhŵynaŵl**

kany, kanny neg. conj. *because … not* 2.4, 2.8, 5.10, 7.4, 9.16; **canys** conj. *because* 2.5, 2.6, 2.10; **kanyt** neg. conj. *because … not* 3.12, 5.1, 6.3, 9.10

kanyat n. *permission* 9.4

cardychŵel adj. *car-returning* 6.3n

carreit n. *carload* 1.1n, 1.5, 1.6

cedor n. *pubic hair* 4.3

keinaŵc, keinhaŵc n. *penny* 1.1n, 1.5, 3.1

ceirch n. pl. *oats* 1.6

keissaŵ, keissiaŵ v.n. *to seek* 1.4, 5.9, 5.10

kenedyl n. *kindred* 6.1, 6.4, 6.5

kerdet v.n. *to value (lit. to walk)*: **kerdet y vreint** grammaticalized phrase *[his] status is valued as, to value his status* 9.1n, 9.2

keuenderŵ n. *cousin* 7.12

cnuf n. *fleece* 1.4
colledic vbl adj. *lost* 2.9
cosp n. *punishment* 3.1
credigaeth n. *creation* 5.8
credu v.n. *to believe* 5.1, 7.13
creireu n. pl. *relics* 5.3, 5.8, 5.10
creus 3 sing. pret. *create* 5.3, 5.8 (v.n. **creu**)
croth n. *womb* 1.2
cussan n. *kiss* 8.2, 8.3, 8.4
cѡbyl adj. *complete, all* 2.3, 3.11
cѡynaѡ v.n. *to complain* 3.10n
cyfelin n. *length [of cloth] measured from the elbow to the wrist or finger* 1.5
kyflauan, kyfulauan n. *a killing, a serious offence* 6.6n, 7.4, 7.7
kyflaѡn adj. *full, complete* 2.3
cyfreideu n. pl. *needs, requirements* 1.4
kyfreith n. *law* 2.2, 2.5, 6.3
kyfreithaѡl adj. *lawful, legal* 5.1, 5.7, 6.2
kyfuranu v.n. *to share, sharing* 7.15
kyhyded n. *equality* 9.8n
kyhyt adj. *as much as* 1.1, 3.2
kymeint adj. *as much as* 9.5, 9.11, 9.12
cymeredic vbl adj. *accepted, affiliated* 9.17
kymeryat n. *acceptance, affiliation* 7.8n
Kymraes n. *Welshwoman* 6.7, 7.6, 9.11
Cymro n. *Welshman* 5.4
kymryt v.n. *to take, to affiliate* 5.7, 7.13, 8.1; **kymer** 3 sing. pres. ind. 7.11, 8.2, 8.4; **cymerer** imps. pres. subj. 9.15; **kymero** 3 sing. pres. subj. 4.5, 5.6; **kymeret** 3 sing. imper. 4.5
kymѡt n. *commote, a land division* 5.10n
cyn prep. *before* 6.6
cynnut n. *fuel, firewood* 1.5, 1.6
cynt adv. *previously* 6.8
kyntaf adj. *first* 1.4, 2.3, 3.3, 9.8
kyny, kynny neg. conj. *although ... not* 4.4, 9.15
kynydu v.n. *increase* 9.13
cysseuyn adj. *first* 1.2, 5.1, 8.1
kyt conj. *although* 7.5

CH

chѡaer n. *sister* 7.14, 7.15

D

da¹ n. *goods* 3.2, 3.11, 7.8, 7.14, 7.15
da² adj. *good* 5.3, 5.8
dauat n. *sheep* 1.4
dauyn n. *drop* 5.8
dat see **tat**
daƀ see **dyuot**
dayaƀc see **tayaƀc**
dec num. *ten* 3.1, 3.4, 3.6
deuach adj. *dark ancestry* [*cattle*] 6.8n
deheu adj. *right* [*hand*] 5.3, 5.8, 8.4
del see **dyuot**
deolef adj. *clamour*: **mab deolef** *son by clamour* 7.1n, 7.2
deruyd 3 sing. habit. pres. ind. *happen*; **darffei** 3 sing. impf. subj. 6.6 (v.n. **darfod**); **o deruyd** *if it happens* [*that*] 5.9n, 5.10, 6.1
deu num. m. *two* 1.5, 5.7, 6.6
deudec num. *twelve* 4.2, 4.6
deugeint num. *forty* [*two twenties*] 4.6, 7.11
deuparth n. *two-thirds* 2.3, 6.4, 6.5, 6.7
deƀisseit adj. *choice, chosen* 1.1
dieissyaƀ v.n. *to compensate, to make good* 2.9
diueichieu v.n. *to give surety, with surety* 6.8
diffeith brenin n. *the king's waste* 9.10n
digaƀn v.n. *to be able to* 7.7, 7.12n, 7.14
diheu adj. *sure, certain, doubtless* 4.6, 9.8, 9.9
dim n. *nothing* 2.8
dimei n. *halfpenny* 1.1n
diodef n. *suffer* 7.3; **mab diodef** *son by sufferance* 7.1n, 7.2, 7.4
diodeuedic vbl adj. *suffered, under sufferance* 9.15
dir n. *necessary, compulsory* 6.8
dirƀy n. *fine* (12 cows or £3) 2.7n
dirƀyus adj. *subject to a fine, liable to a fine* 3.10
diƀc 3 sing. pres. ind. *compensate, make good* 7.15; **diƀycko** 3 sing. pres. subj. 7.7n (v.n. **diwyn**)
diƀethaf adj. *last* 2.3, 8.3, 8.4
dodi v.n. *to put* 5.3; **dyt** 3 sing. pres. ind. 2.10
dracheuyn see **tracheuyn**
dri see **tri**
dros prep. *over, on behalf of* 4.4; **drostaƀ** 3 sing. m. 2.7, 2.10, 3.2
dƀy num. f. *two* 1.5, 9.4
dƀylaƀ n. *dual hands* 8.2

dỽyn v.n. *to take* 3.6; *to affiliate [legally]* 5.1n, 5.2, 5.4, 5.5, 5.6, 6.2, 6.6; **dỽc** 3 sing. pres. ind. 6.2; **dyccer** imps. pres. subj. 5.1, 6.1; **dycco** 3 sing. pres. subj. 7.2, 7.3, 8.1, 9.15

dyd n. *day* 7.3

dyuot v.n. ('dod') *to come* 5.3, 5.6, 5.8, 9.16; **daỽ** 3 sing. pres. ind. 4.3, 6.7; **del** 3 sing. pres. subj. 3.5

dyfỽr n. *water* 5.6

dygỽyd v.n. *to happen, to pass into* 9.4; **dygỽydo** 3 sing. pres. subj. 7.12n

dygyn n. *end point* 7.2n

dygyngoll n. *dire loss* 6.5n

dylyet n. *entitlement, inheritance* 9.4

dylyu v.n. *to be obliged to/be entitled to* 6.6, 9.1, 9.2; **dyly** 3 sing. pres. ind. 1.4, 2.8, 2.9; **dylyant** 3 pl. pres. ind. 2.7, 9.8; **dylyir** imps. pres. ind. 1.2n, 2.1, 2.2; **dylyo** 3 sing. pres. subj. 9.10

dyn n. *man* 2.6, 2.8, 6.7

dyrchauo 3 sing. pres. subj. *increase, raise* 9.13 (v.n. **dyrchafu**)

dyry 3 sing. pres. ind. *give* 1.4 (v.n. **dyroddi**)

dyỽedassam 1 pl. pret. *say* 5.8, 6.9; **dyỽeit** 3 sing. pres. ind. 2.2, 2.4, 2.5; **dyỽespỽyt** imps. pret. 1.1, 5.6n; **dyỽetter** imps. pres. subj. 9.14; **dyỽetto** 3 sing. pres. subj. 7.2 (v.n. **dyỽedud**)

E

ebediỽ n. *death-duty* 3.4n, 9.13

ef¹ 3 sing. m. indep. pers. pron. 2.10, 3.3, 3.10

ef² 3 sing. m. aff. pron. 2.10, 3.5, 5.6

eglỽys n. *church* 5.3 5.6 5.8 7.9

ehag n. *broad, wide* ('eang') 7.4n

ehun 3 sing. pron. *himself, herself* 2.10, 3.3, 3.5; **ehunan** 3 sing. pron. *himself, herself* 4.4; **eu hun** 8.1

eidaỽ n. *property, goods* 2.9

eidaỽ 3 sing. m. poss. pron. *his* 3.2; **eidi** 3 sing. f. poss. pron. *her* 4.3, 4.4; **eidunt** 3 pl. poss. pron. *their* 9.16

eil ord. num. *second* 8.4

eill 3 sing. pres. ind. *be able to* 6.1, 6.2, 7.9; **ellir** imps. pres. ind. *may* 7.2 (v.n. **gallu**)

eilỽeith adv. *a second time* 6.2, 8.2

eithyr prep. *but, except* 2.7

el 3 sing. pres. subj. *go* 2.7 (v.n. **mynd, myned**)

eneit n. *soul, life* 2.3

enỽ n. *name* 2.6 5.3

er prep. *for, for the sake of* 7.13

erbyn prep. *by* 5.3, 8.4

ereill pl. pron. *others* 7.13, 9.9; see also **arall**
erioet adv. *ever, never* 5.8
estraѡn n. *foreigner* 3.9
etiued n. *heir* 3.11
etrych v.n. *to see* 9.1
eu 3 pl. poss. pron. *their* 6.6, 7.15, 8.1

V

vaeddu see **maeddu**
val prep. *like, as* 1.2, 5.2, 5.5
vara see **bara**
vedyd, vedydyer see **bedyd, bedydyer**
vedho 3 sing. pres. subj. *own, possess* 3.1, 4.3, 4.4 (v.n. **meddu**)
veicheu, veichiѡs, veichiѡys see **meichiaѡ**
veithrin see **meithrin**
velly adv. *thus, so, in this way* 5.3, 5.4, 5.8
vlith see **blith**
vlѡydyn see **blѡydyn**
vo, vot, vu, vyd see **bot**
voned n. *lineage* 3.12
vraѡt see **braѡt**
vreint see **breint**
vrethyn see **brethyn**
vry adv. *above* 1.1
vut see **mut**
vynn, vynner, vynno see **mynn**
vyth see **byth**
vyѡ see **byѡ**

G

gaffel see **kaffel**
galanas n. *life-value, fine for homicide* 2.1n, 2.2, 2.3
galhon see **calhon**
gelѡir imps. pres. ind. *call* 6.8 (v.n. **galw**)
gan prep. *from, by, with, on account of* 1.1, 3.10, 4.5, 7.9, 7.13; **gantaѡ** 3 sing. m. 2.8, 7.9, 9.1; **genti** 3 sing. f. 1.4
ganher see **geni**
ganyat see **kanyat**
geir n. *word* 9.7n
geni v.n. *to be born* 9.1, 9.6; **ganer** imps. pres. subj. 1.3, 3.1, 3.3, 4.2; **ganet** imps. pret. 9.6
gilyd: y gilydd prep. *each other* 7.12

glan adj. *clean, pure* 7.9
gnottaf adj. spv. *most usual, most customary* 7.13n
gobyr n. *reward, payment* 7.13n
gorchymyn n. *order, command* 3.6
goreu adj. spv. *best* 1.1
goreugῤyr n. *best men* 7.9, 7.10, 8.4
gredigaeth see **credigaeth**
greus see **creus**
gussan see **cussan**
gῤadu v.n. *to deny* 5.1, 5.7, 5.8; **gῤata** 3 sing. pres. ind. 7.6, 7.10, 7.11; **gῤattei** 3 sing. impf. subj. 7.9; **gῤedir** imps. pres. ind. 9.17; **gῤadῤys** 3 sing. pret. 6.2, 6.3; **gῤadῤyt** imps. pret. 7.4, 9.15; **gῤatter** imps. pres. subj. 7.6, 9.13
gῤaet n. *blood* 5.8
gῤahanῤys 3 sing. pret. *separate* 5.8 (v.n. gwahanu)
gῤarthec n. pl. *cattle* 6.8n; see also **deuach**
gῤbyl see **cῤbyl**
gῤed n. *yoke* 2.10, 7.9
gῤedy conj. *after* 1.3, 3.5, 4.1; **gῤedy as** with syllabic obj. pron. 8.1
gῤeithret n. *act* 2.8
gῤenith n. *wheat* 1.5, 1.6
gῤeren n. *tallow-cake* 1.5
gῤerth n. *value, a price* 6.9, 7.13
gῤneuthur v.n. *to do, to accomplish* 1.5, 5.7, 6.6, 7.4; **gῤna** 3 sing. pres. ind. 3.10; **gῤnel** 3 sing. pres. subj. 6.3; **gῤnelῤynt** 3 pl. pres. subj. 7.15
gῤr n. *man* 2.4, 2.5, 5.3; **gῤyr** n. pl. *men* 7.11, 8.3, 8.4
gῤreic n. *woman* 1.1n, 2.4, 7.3
gῤrhav v.n. *to pay homage* 3.7n
gῤybot v.n. *to know* 9.6; **gῤyr** 3 sing. pres. ind. 7.11, 8.4; **gῤypper** imps. pres. subj. 9.8; **gῤyppo** 3 sing. pres. subj. 9.9; **gῤybydir** imps. habit. pres. 2.6; **gῤys** imps. pres. 2.4
gῤydua n. *burial-place* 5.3n
gῤyn adj. *white* 1.5, 2.3
gῤynaῤ see **cῤynaῤ**
gyfelin see **cyfelin**
gyfreideu see **cyfreideu**
gyfreith, gyfreithaῤl see **kyfreith**
gyfulauan see **kyflauan**
gyhyt see **kyhyt**
gymeredic see **cymeredic**
gynnut see **cynnut**
gynt see **cynt**
gyrru v.n. *to drive* 7.12n
gysseuyn, gyssefin see **cysseuyn**

H

hagen conj. *however* 2.9
hanner n. *half* 9.8
hayarn n. *iron* 1.5
heb prep. *without* 4.6
heuyt adv. *also* 4.6
heid n. *barley* 1.6
herwyd conj. *according to* 2.6, 7.11, 9.1
hi 3 sing. f. aff. pron. *her* 1.3, 1.7, 4.3
hitheu 3 sing. f. conjv. pron. *her* 5.10, 6.2
hoen see **oen**
holi v.n. *to claim* 1.4, 2.6n, 3.2; **holer** imps. pres. subj. 2.6, 3.8
holl pron. *all, the whole* 1.4, 3.2
honno 3 sing. f. dem. pron. *that* 5.3, 5.8
hugeint see **ugeint**
hun see **ehun**
hwnn 3 sing. m. dem. pron. *this* 3.1
hwnnw 3 sing. m. dem. pron. *that* 3.12, 5.3, 5.8
hwy 3 pl. aff. poss. pron. *their* 6.6, 9.16
hwynt¹ 3 pl. aff. pers. pron. *their, them* 7.9
hwynt² 3 pl. indep. pers. pron. *them* 7.15
hwynteu 3 pl. conjv. aff. pron. *them* 9.8
hymduc see **ymdwyn**
hyn 3 pl. dem. pron. *these* 1.2, 5.2, 5.5, 8.1
hynaf adj. spv. *eldest, most senior* 8.3, 8.4
hynny dem. pron. *that, those* 1.1, 1.3, 2.3
hyt, hyt ar prep. *until, as far as* 5.3, 5.9, 9.14; **hyt at** *as far as, to* 8.3, 8.4; **hyt pan** *until* 2.7, 4.1; **hyt ym penn** *until, up to* (+ age in years) 4.6; **hyt yr** *to, as far as* 5.3, 5.6, 5.8

I

i aff. poss. pron. *my* 5.3
iawn¹ adj. *right, correct* 3.7, 5.7, 5.8, 9.6; **iawnach** adj. comp. *more right* 2.4; **iawnaf** adj. spv. *most right* 2.5, 7.13
iawn² n. *right, compensation* 3.10 (+ with forms of 'gwneud', *to make*)
idaw 3 sing. m. prep. *to him* 1.4, 1.5, 3.6
idi 3 sing. f. prep. *to her* 1.3, 4.3, 4.6
ieuaf adj. spv. *youngest* 9.6, 9.9
iwt n. *porridge* 1.5

L

lan see **glan**

Ll

llad v.n. *to kill* 6.4, 6.6, 6.7; **lledir** imps. pres. ind. 6.5
llaw n. *hand* 2.10, 5.3, 5.8
lle n. *place* 1.3, 3.11, 7.14, 8.4
lleueryd see **tauot leueryd**
llo n. *calf* 1.6
llofrud n. *homicide [person]* 6.4, 6.6, 6.7
llw n. *oath* 4.1, 4.6, 5.9, 7.9, 7.13

M

mab n. *son, male* 1.1, 1.2, 1.5; **meibon** n. pl. *sons* 9.5
mac see **magu**
mae see **bot**
maeddu v.n. *to beat, to strike* 3.9; **maed** 3 sing. pres. ind. 3.10
maent see **bot**
maeth: mab maeth adj. *foster son* 9.4, 9.5; see also **meithrin**
magu v.n. *to rear, to grow* 1.1, 1.2, 9.4; **mac** 3 sing. pres. ind. 1.3
mal prep. *like, as* 9.13
mam n. *mother* 1.2, 5.3, 5.8
marchawc n. *knight* 3.12
marw[1] adj. *dead* 3.3, 3.11, 3.12, 9.4, 9.17
marw[2] v.n. *to die* 7.9
marwty n. *dead-house* 3.2n, 3.11
megys conj. *as, just as* 5.6
meicheu n. *surety* 4.5n
meichiaw v.n. *to give surety* 6.6; **veichwys** 3 sing. pret. 6.6 (v.n. **meichio**)
meithrin n. *to rear, to nurse* 7.8, 9.4n
merch n. *daughter* 4.1, 4.4, 9.10, 9.12
mis n. *month* 1.2, 1.3, 2.3
mlyned see **blwydyn**
muneit n. *handful* 1.5
mut adj. *mute* 9.16
mwy adj. comp. *more* 3.9
mynet v.n. *to go* 4.1; **a** 3 sing. pres. ind. 3.3, 3.12
mynn 3 sing. pres. ind. *want, wish* 1.7, 4.4, 5.8, 7.7, 7.15; **mynnant** 3 pl. pres. ind. 9.16; **mynner** imps. pres. subj. 7.2; **vynno** 3 sing. pres. subj. 5.1, 5.2 (v.n. **mynnu**)

N

na¹, nat¹ vbl neg. part. *not* 2.7, 3.11, 3.12
na ... na neg. conj. *neither ... nor* 2.7, 7.11
na'e neg. part. with 3 sing. m. inf. poss. pron. *nor his* 9.16
nac neg. conj. *nor* 2.7, 7.13
namyn conj. *except* 3.1, 3.2, 3.12
naƀ num. *nine* 1.2
neb pron. *nobody, somebody, whoever* 3.1, 3.12, 4.5
neill pron. *one, this* 9.8
nessaf adj. *next* 8.4
neu conj. *or* 1.5, 7.15
ni aff. pers. pron. *we, us* 5.8, 6.9
noc conj. *than* 2.4, 3.9
noe n. *platter, dish*: ƀrth noe y tat *dependent on his father* 3.1n, 4.2, 4.4
ny, nyt neg. part. *not* 2.6, 3.1, 3.4; **nys** with sing. inf. obj. pron. 7.2

O

o¹ prep. *from, of* 1.5, 1.6, 2.3; **ohonaƀ** 3 sing. m. 3.10, 6.7, 7.5; **ohonunt** 3 pl. 9.6; **o'e** with 3 sing. m. inf. poss. pron. *of his* 3.10, 4.4, 5.8; **o'r** with def. art. *of the* 1.1, 2.9, 3.12
o² conj. *if* 6.5, 6.6, 9.3; **o'r** (with affirm. part. 'ry') 3.1, 3.3, 3.11
o deruyd see **deruyd**
odyna adv. *then, thence* 1.4, 1.5, 4.6
oen n. *lamb* 1.4
oes n. *age [period of time]* 2.8, 3.12, 5.8, 6.7, 9.10
oet n. *time, appointed time* 3.12, 4.3, 5.9, 5.10
offeren n. *mass* 5.6
ol see **yn ol**
oll adj. *all* 1.7, 9.4
ony conj. *unless* 7.10, 7.11, 7.12; **onyt** 4.4, 5.8, 7.14, 7.15; **onys** with 3 sing. m. inf. obj. pron. 9.16; with 3 pl. inf. obj. pron. 1.7
os conj. *if* 4.5, 5.8, 7.6 (o² + 'ys', 3 sing. pres. ind. of **bot**); with 3 pl. inf. obj. pron. 1.7; with 3 sing. m. inf. obj. pron. 3.10

P

pa pron. *which* 5.2, 9.1; for **pa ... bynnag** see **bynnac**
pan conj. *when* 2.2, 2.7, 3.1; **pan yƀ** (with 'yƀ' 3 sing. pres. ind. of **bot**) *that it is* 2.2n, 6.6, 9.10
patell n. *dish, pan* 1.1, 1.5
pedeir num. f. *four* 1.1, 1.5, 3.1
pedrussaƀ v.n. *to doubt, to be uncertain* 2.1; see also **petrus**

98   GLOSSARY

peis n. *tunic* 1.1n
penn n. *head* 5.3, 5.8; **ym penn** prep. *at the end of [period of time]* 3.6, 4.6; **o benn** prep. *from the end of [period of time]* 2.10
pennaf adj. *chief, main* 2.5
pennkenedyl n. *head of kindred* 7.9n, 7.10, 7.11, 8.2, 8.3, 8.4
perchennaѡc n. *owner* 9.10
perued n. *middle* 2.3
periglaѡr n. *parish priest* 2.10
perthyn v.n. *belong to, pertain to* 1.1
peth¹ n. *thing* 2.5, 3.2, 3.8, 5.1, 5.7
peth² interr. pron. *what, which* 2.1, 2.4
petrus adj. *uncertain* 9.1; see also **pedrussaѡ**
plant n. pl. *children, offspring* 4.6, 9.4, 9.5, 9.6
pob, pop pron. *all, every* 2.6, 3.2, 3.8
pryt ... na neg. conj. *since ... not* 4.6
pѡy pron. *who* 5.1, 9.6, 9.8
pѡyll n. *sense, understanding* 2.8
py pron. *which* 9.1

R

rac prep. *lest, in case of* 7.14, 7.15, 9.15
rannu v.n. *to share, to divide* 7.14; **renir** imps. pres. ind. 9.8
rei pron. *some* 2.1, 2.4, 7.13, 9.1
reit n. *necessity, must* 5.1, 9.16
rodi v.n. *to give* 4.3, 4.4, 5.8; **ryd** 3 sing. pres. ind. 4.5; **rodir** imps. pres. ind. 6.7; **rother** imps. pres. subj. 1.7
rodyat n. *giver* 4.4
rud adj. *red* 2.3
rѡg prep. *among, between* 8.2; **rydunt** 3 pl. 9.7, 9.8
ry, re affirm. part. 5.3, 5.8
ryd see **rodi**
rydunt see **rѡg**

S

sarhaet n. *payment/compensation for deliberate act* 3.10n, 6.9
sef part. *this/that is* 2.3, 6.2, 7.2, 8.2, 9.2, 9.15
seith num. *seven* 2.7, 4.1, 7.9
seithuet ord. num. *seventh* 2.10; **ar y seithvet** (with prep. 'ar', *one of seven*) 7.9, 8.2
sѡyn n. *holy* 5.6

T

tauot leueryd n. *by word of mouth (lit. tongue-speech)* 7.2n
tal n. *payment* 6.8
talu v.n. *to pay* 2.4, 2.7, 2.10; **talo** 3 sing. pres. subj. 1.1n, 6.7; **tal** 3 sing. pres. ind. 3.5, 6.4; **telit** imps. past subj. 6.8
tat n. *father* 1.1, 1.4, 2.10
tayaƀc n. *villein* 9.4; **tayogeu** n. pl. *villeins* 1.1n
tebygu v.n. *to believe, to suppose* 9.14
teir num. f. *three* 9.4
tir n. *land* 1.1, 7.12
torllƀyth n. *litter, pregnancy* 9.6, 9.8
tra conj. *while* 6.6
tracheuyn adv. *afterwards, again* 6.3
trannoeth adv. *the next day* 5.9, 7.7
trayan n. *a third, a third part* 2.3, 6.4, 6.7
tref: tref tat, tref y tat n. *patrimony, share of land* 7.13n, 9.2, 9.3
tri num. m. *three* 1.3, 1.6, 2.3, 6.5
tridieu n. pl. *three days* 5.10
trydyd ord. num. *third* 6.7, 7.8
ty n. *house* 3.11
tydyn n. *toft, homestead, smallholding* 9.6n, 9.8
tyfo 3 sing. pres. subj. *grow* 1.1 (v.n. **tyfu**)
tygu v.n. *to swear* 2.7, 2.10, 5.3, 5.8

U/V

uchaf see **ychaf**
vchelƀr n. *nobleman* 9.4
vchot adv. *above* 5.6, 5.8, 6.9
ugeint num. *twenty* 7.1, 8.4, 9.11, 9.12
vn num. *one* 1.5, 2.4, 3.1

ƀ

ƀadu, ƀadƀyt see **gƀadu**
ƀaet see **gƀaet**
ƀarthec see **gƀarthec**
ƀed see **gƀed**
ƀedy see **gƀedy**
ƀeithion adv. *now, from now on* 6.4n
ƀeithret see **gƀeithret**
ƀerth see **gƀerth**
ƀna, ƀnel, ƀnelƀynt, ƀneuthur see **gƀneuthur**

ỽrth prep. *by, beside, according to* 3.1, 3.7, 4.2
ỽrth hynny conjv. advl phrase *because, because of that* 2.6, 2.7, 9.7
ỽrth vot, ỽrth y vot conjv. advl phrase *because* 6.8, 7.4,
ỽrth na, ỽrth nad neg. conjv. advl phrase *because there is not* 6.7, 9.15
ỽydua see **gỽydua**
ỽynebỽerth n. *honour-price* 2.1n
ỽypper, ỽyppo see **gỽybot**
ỽyr see **gỽr, gỽyr**
ỽys see **gỽybot**
ỽynt, ỽynteu, ỽy see **hỽynteu, hỽynt^{1}, hỽynt^{2}, hỽy**

Y

y^{1} def. art. *the* 1.1, 1.2, 1.5; see also **yr**
y^{2} 3 sing. m. pref. poss. pron. *his* 1.4, 2.6, 3.1; 3 sing. f. pref. poss. pron. *her* 1.2, 4.4, 7.14
y^{3} prep. *to, for* 1.5, 1.7, 4.3; **y'r** with def. art. 2.7, 5.3, 5.7; **y'm** with poss. 5.3; **y'r** with def. art. 2.7, 3.7, 5.7
y^{4} pvbl part. 1.3, 1.4, 2.3; see also **yd**
y^{5} rel. part. *which, that, when, where, who* 3.3, 5.3, 5.6, 7.12
y gan see **gan**
ychaf adj. spv. ('uchaf') *highest* 9.2
ychen n. pl. *oxen* 1.5
yd pvbl part. 9.1, 9.2; see also y^{4}
yg n. ('ing') *strait, rough time* 7.4n
ygneit n. pl. *justices* 9.9
ym for **ym penn** see **penn**
ymdanaỽ 1 sing. m. prep. *for him* 2.4; see also **am**
ymdỽyn v.n. *to conceive, to become pregnant* 4.6; **[h]ymduc** 3 sing. pres. ind. with aspiration after 3 sing. inf. pron. *carries him* 1.2n
ymreint see **breint**
ymyrru *take action* 9.17n; see also **gyrru**
yn^{1} part. with v.n. 2.1, 3.2, 3.3
yn^{2} prep. *in* 1.2, 1.3, 2.3; **yndaỽ** 3 sing. m. 5.8; **yndi** 3 sing. f. 5.3, 5.6
yn^{3} adv. part. 1.4, 2.5, 3.11
yn ol prep. *according to* 2.5; prep. *back, behind, after* 9.8
yna adv. *then, at that time, there* 2.10, 3.3, 3.7
yndaỽ see **yn^{2}**
yndi see **yn^{2}**
ynvyt adj. *mentally unstable* 2.8
ynt see **bot**
ynteu^{1} 3 sing. m. aff. pron. 2.8, 3.12, 5.6
ynteu^{2} indep. pron. 4.5

yny conj. *until* 2.5, 2.6, 3.1
yr (before vowels) def. art. *the* 3.6, 3.7, 3.10; see also **y**[1]
yr prep. *in order to, because of* 1.1, 7.7, 7.12, 7.13
yrru see **gyrru**
ysgynno 3 sing. pres. subj. *ascend, mount* [*horse*] 3.12n (v.n. **esgyn, ysgyn**)
yssyd see **bot**
yt n. *corn* 1.1
yѵ see **bot**

Personal or Place Names

Adaf *Adam* 5.8
Duѵ *God* 2.10, 5.3, 5.8
Poѵys *Powys* [*territory*] 7.11

BIBLIOGRAPHY

Manuscript Sources

Aberystwyth, National Library of Wales, Peniarth MS 29, 'The Black Book of Chirk'
Aberystwyth, National Library of Wales, Peniarth MS 30
Aberystwyth, National Library of Wales, Peniarth MS 32
Aberystwyth, National Library of Wales, Peniarth MS 34
Aberystwyth, National Library of Wales, Peniarth MS 35
Aberystwyth, National Library of Wales, Peniarth MS 39
Aberystwyth, National Library of Wales, Peniarth MS 40
Aberystwyth, National Library of Wales, Wynnstay MS 36
Cambridge, Corpus Christi College, MS 454
London, British Library, Add. MS 14,931
London, British Library, Add. MS 22,356
London, British Library, Cotton MS Caligula A III
London, British Library, Cotton MS Titus D III
London, British Library, Cotton MS Vespasian E XI
Oxford, Bodleian Library, MS Rawlinson C. 821
Oxford, Jesus College, MS 57
Oxford, Jesus College, MS 111, 'The Red Book of Hergest'

Printed Primary and Secondary Sources

Anderson, Katharine, '*Urth Noe e Tat*: The Question of Fosterage in High Medieval Wales', *North American Journal of Welsh Studies*, 4.1 (2004), pp. 1–11
Ariès, Philippe, *Centuries of Childhood* (Pimlico, 1973)
Cartwright, Jane, *Hystoria Gweryddon yr Almaen: The Middle Welsh Life of St Ursula and the 11,000 Virgins*, MHRA Library of Medieval Welsh Literature, 5 (MHRA, 2020)
Charles-Edwards, T. M., *Early Irish and Welsh Kinship* (Oxford University Press, 1993)
—— '*Nei, keifn*, and *kefynderw*', *Bulletin of the Board of Celtic Studies*, 25.4 (1972–74), pp. 386–88
—— 'The Seven Bishop-Houses of Dyfed', *Bulletin of the Board of Celtic Studies*, 24.3 (1970–72), pp. 247–62
—— 'Some Celtic Kinship Terms', *Bulletin of the Board of Celtic Studies*, 24.2 (1970–72), pp. 105–22
—— 'The Textual Tradition of Llyfr Iorwerth Revisited, or Why Both J. Gwenogvryn Evans and Daniel Huws May Be Right', in *Cyfarwydd Mewn Cyfraith: Studies in Honour of Morfydd E. Owen*, ed. by Sara Elin Roberts, Simon Rodway, and Alexander Falileyev, Welsh Legal History Society, 17 (Welsh Legal History Society, 2022), pp. 21–45
—— *Wales and the Britons, 350–1064* (Oxford University Press, 2012)

—— *The Welsh Laws* (Writers of Wales) (University of Wales Press, 1989)

——, Morfydd E. Owen, and Paul Russell (eds), *The Welsh King and his Court* (University of Wales Press, 2000)

——, Morfydd E. Owen, and Dafydd B. Walters (eds), *Lawyers and Laymen: Studies in the History of Law Presented to Professor Dafydd Jenkins on his Seventy-Fifth Birthday, Gŵyl Ddewi 1986* (University of Wales Press, 1986)

——, and Paul Russell (eds), *Tair Colofn Cyfraith. The Three Columns of Law in Medieval Wales: Homicide, Theft and Fire*, Welsh Legal History Society, 5 (Welsh Legal History Society, 2005)

Comeau, Rhiannon, and Steve Burrow, 'Corn-Drying Kilns in Wales: A Review of the Evidence', *Archaeologia Cambrensis*, 170 (2021), pp. 111–49

Davies, R. R., 'Law and National Identity in Thirteenth-Century Wales', in *Welsh Society and Nationhood: Historical Essays Presented to Glanmor Williams*, ed. by R. R. Davies (University of Wales Press, 1984), pp. 51–69

Elias, G. Angharad, 'Llawysgrif Peniarth 164 a Pharhad Cyfraith Hywel yn yr Oesoedd Canol Diweddar', *Llên Cymru*, 33 (2010), pp. 32–50

—— *Yr Ail Lyfr Du o'r Waun. Golygiad Beirniadol ac Eglurhaol o Lsgr. Peniarth 164 (H)*, Texts and Studies in Medieval Welsh Law, 5, 2 vols (Seminar Cyfraith Hywel, 2018)

Emanuel, Hywel D., 'Blegywryd and the Welsh Laws', *Bulletin of the Board of Celtic Studies*, 20.3 (1962–64), pp. 256–60

—— 'The Book of Blegywryd and MS. Rawlinson 821', in *Celtic Law Papers*, ed. by Dafydd Jenkins (Les Editions de la Librairie Encyclopédique, 1973), pp. 161–70

—— *The Latin Texts of the Welsh Laws* (University of Wales Press, 1967)

—— 'Llyfr Blegywryd a Llawysgrif Rawlinson 821', *Bulletin of the Board of Celtic Studies*, 19.1 (1960–62), 23–28

Eska, Charlene M., *Cáin Lánamna: An Old Irish Tract on Marriage and Divorce Law* (Brill, 2010)

Evans, D. Simon, *Gramadeg Cymraeg Canol* (University of Wales Press, 1951)

—— *A Grammar of Middle Welsh* (Dublin Institute for Advanced Studies, 1964)

Goodman, R. T., '"In a Father's Place": Anglo-Saxon Kingship and Masculinity in the Long Tenth Century' (unpublished doctoral thesis, University of Manchester, 2018) <https://research.manchester.ac.uk/en/studentTheses/in-a-fathers-place-anglo-saxon-kingship-and-masculinity-in-the-lo>

Griffiths, Ralph A., 'Gruffydd ap Nicholas and the Fall of the House of Lancaster', *Welsh History Review*, 2.3 (1965), pp. 213–31

—— 'Gruffydd ap Nicholas and the Rise of the House of Dinefwr', *National Library of Wales Journal*, 13.3 (1964), pp. 256–65

Hughes, Ian, *Math uab Mathonwy: The Fourth Branch of the Mabinogi* (Dublin Institute for Advanced Studies, 2013)

Huws, Daniel, *Medieval Welsh Manuscripts* (University of Wales Press, 2000)

—— *A Repertory of Welsh Manuscripts and Scribes, c.800–c.1800* (National Library of Wales, 2022)

James, Christine, 'Llyfr Cyfraith o Ddyffryn Teifi: Disgrifiad o BL. Add. 22,356', *National Library of Wales Journal*, 27.1 (1991), pp. 383–404

—— *Machlud Cyfraith Hywel: Golygiad Beirniadol ac Eglurhaol o Lsgr. BL Add. 22356 (S)*, Texts and Studies in Medieval Welsh Law (Seminar Cyfraith Hywel, 2013) <http://cyfraith-hywel.org.uk/cy/machlud-cyf-hyw.php>

—— 'Parhad, Pragmatiaeth, Propaganda: Llawysgrifau Cyfraith Hywel yn yr Oesoedd Canol Diweddar', *Cof Cenedl*, 22 (2007), pp. 33–67

—— 'Tradition and Innovation in Some Later Medieval Welsh Lawbooks', *Bulletin of the Board of Celtic Studies*, 40 (1993), pp. 148–56

Jenkins, Dafydd, *Agricultural Co-operation in Welsh Medieval Law* (Amgueddfa Werin Cymru, 1982)

—— *Cyfraith Hywel: Rhagarweiniad i Gyfraith Gynhenid Cymru'r Oesau Canol* (Gomer, 1970)

—— *Damweiniau Colan* (Cymdeithas Llyfrau Ceredigion, 1973)

—— 'A Family of Medieval Welsh Lawyers', in *Celtic Law Papers*, ed. by Dafydd Jenkins (Les Editions de la Librairie Encyclopédique, 1973), pp. 121–33

—— 'Iorwerth ap Madog: Gŵr Cyfraith o'r Drydedd Ganrif Ar Ddeg', *National Library of Wales Journal*, 8.2 (1953), pp. 164–70

—— 'Iorwerth ap Madog a Hywel Dda': Review of *Llyfr Iorwerth: A Critical Text of the 'Venedotian Code' of Medieval Welsh Law*, *Lleufer*, 17.1 (1961), pp. 17–33

—— *The Law of Hywel Dda: Law Texts from Medieval Wales* (Gomer, 1986)

—— *Llyfr Colan* (University of Wales Press, 1963)

—— 'The Significance of the Law of Hywel', *Transactions of the Honourable Society of the Cymmrodorion*, 1977, pp. 54–76

—— 'Yr Ynad Coch', *Bulletin of the Board of Celtic Studies*, 22.1 (1966–68), pp. 345–46

——, and Morfydd E. Owen (eds), *The Welsh Law of Women* (University of Wales Press, 1980)

Kelly, Fergus, *Early Irish Farming* (Dublin Institute for Advanced Studies, 2000)

—— *A Guide to Early Irish Law* (Dublin Institute for Advanced Studies, 1988)

Lloyd, J. E., 'Hywel Dda: The Historical Setting', *Aberystwyth Studies X: The Hywel Dda Millenary Volume* (1928), pp. 1–4

Maund, Kari, *The Welsh Kings: The Medieval Rulers of Wales* (Tempus, 2000)

McAll, C., 'The Normal Paradigms of a Woman's Life in the Irish and Welsh Texts', in *The Welsh Law of Women*, ed. by Dafydd Jenkins and Morfydd E. Owen (University of Wales Press, 1980), pp. 7–22

Mondon, Jean-Francois R., *Cymraec Canawl: An Introduction to Middle Welsh* (Lincom, 2020)

Ní Chonaill, Bronagh, 'Contentious Kinship: The Penumbra of Established Kinship in Medieval Irish Law', in *Tome: Studies in Medieval Celtic History and Law in Honour of Thomas Charles-Edwards*, ed. by Fiona Edmunds and Paul Russell (The Boydell Press, 2001), pp. 173–82

Nic Eoin, Máirín, 'From Childhood Vulnerability to Adolescent Delinquency: Literary Sources for the History of Childhood in Medieval Ireland', *Studia Hibernica*, 38 (2012), pp. 9–35

Orme, Nicholas, *Going to Church in Medieval England* (Yale University Press, 2021)

—— *Medieval Children* (Yale University Press, 2001)

Owen, Aneurin, *Ancient Laws and Institutes of Wales*, 2 vols (Public Records Commission, 1841)

Owen, Morfydd E., 'A Fifteenth-Century Lawbook from Cefnllys', *Transactions of the Radnorshire Society*, 81 (2011), pp. 77–93

—— 'Functional Prose: Religion, Science, Grammar, Law', in *A Guide to Welsh*

Literature Vol. 1, ed. by A. O. H. Jarman and G. R. Hughes (University of Wales Press, 1992), pp. 248–76
—— 'Gwŷr Dysg Yr Oesoedd Canol', *Ysgrifau Beirniadol*, 17 (1990), pp. 42–62
—— 'Medics and Medicine', in *The Welsh King and his Court*, ed. by T. M. Charles-Edwards, Morfydd E. Owen, and Paul Russell (University of Wales Press, 2000), pp. 116–141
—— 'Shame and Reparation: Women's Place in the Kin', in *The Welsh Law of Women*, ed. by Dafydd Jenkins and Morfydd E. Owen (University of Wales Press, 1980), pp. 40–68
Parkes, Peter, 'Celtic Fosterage: Adoptive Kinship and Clientage in Northwest Europe', *Comparative Studies in Society and History*, 48.2 (2006), pp. 359–95
Penn, Michael, 'Performing Family: Ritual Kissing and the Construction of Early Christian Kinship', *Journal of Early Christian Studies*, 10.2 (2002), pp. 151–74
Petrovskaia, Natalia I., *Delw y Byd: A Medieval Welsh Encyclopaedia*, MHRA Library of Medieval Welsh Literature, 6 (MHRA, 2020)
Preston-Matto, Lahney, '"I Would Like to Make It Up to You by Fostering your Son": Fosterage and Fixing Relations in Medieval Iceland', in *Kids Those Days: Children in Medieval Culture*, ed. by Lahney Preston-Matto and Mary A. Valante (Brill, 2022), pp. 109–26
Pryce, Huw, 'The Context and Purpose of the Earliest Welsh Lawbooks', *Cambrian Medieval Celtic Studies*, 39 (2000), pp. 39–63
—— 'Lawbooks and Literacy in Medieval Wales', *Speculum*, 75.1 (2000), pp. 29–67
—— 'Medieval Welsh Law', *Newsletter of the School of Celtic Studies* (Dublin Institute of Advanced Studies), 4 (1990), pp. 30–34
—— *Native Law and the Church in Medieval Wales* (Oxford University Press, 1993)
—— 'The Prologues to the Welsh Lawbooks', *Bulletin of the Board of Celtic Studies*, 33 (1986), pp. 151–82
Richards, Melville, *Cyfreithiau Hywel Dda yn ôl Llawysgrif Coleg yr Iesu LVII*, 2nd edn (University of Wales Press, 1990)
—— *The Laws of Hywel Dda* (Liverpool University Press, 1954)
Roberts, Richard Glyn, *Diarhebion Llyfr Coch Hergest* (CMCS, 2013)
Roberts, Sara Elin, 'Addysg Broffesiynol yng Nghymru yn yr Oesoedd Canol: Y Beirdd a'r Cyfreithwyr', *Llên Cymru*, 26 (2003), pp. 1–17
—— 'Bells, Bulls, and Bushes: Secret Sex in the Laws', in *Cyfarwydd Mewn Cyfraith: Studies in Honour of Morfydd E. Owen*, ed. by Sara Elin Roberts, Simon Rodway, and Alexander Falileyev, Welsh Legal History Society, 17 (Welsh Legal History Society, 2022), pp. 112–23
—— '"By the Authority of the Devil": The Operation of Welsh and English Law in Medieval Wales', in *Authority and Subjugation in the Writing of Medieval Wales*, ed. by Simon Meecham-Jones and Ruth Kennedy (Palgrave Macmillan, 2008), pp. 85–97
—— 'Creu Trefn o Anhrefn: Gwaith Copïydd Testun Cyfreithiol', *National Library of Wales Journal*, 32.4 (2002), pp. 397–420
—— 'Emerging from the Bushes: The Welsh Law of Women and the Legal Triads', in *Law, Literature and Society: CSANA Yearbook 7*, ed. by Joe F. Eska (Four Courts Press, 2008), pp. 58–76
—— *The Growth of Law in Medieval Wales, c.1100–c.1500* (The Boydell Press, 2022)
—— '"Gwreic wyf fi": Transition to Womanhood in Medieval Wales', in *Middle-*

Aged Women in the Middle Ages, ed. by Sue Niebrzydowski (D. S. Brewer, 2011), pp. 25–36

—— 'The Iorwerth Triads', in *Tome: Studies in Medieval Celtic History and Law in Honour of Thomas Charles-Edwards*, ed. by Fiona Edmonds and Paul Russell (The Boydell Press, 2011), pp. 155–74

—— *The Legal Triads of Medieval Wales* (University of Wales Press, 2007)

—— *Llawysgrif Pomffred: An Edition and Study of Peniarth MS 259B* (Brill, 2011)

—— 'Plaints in Welsh Mediaeval Law', *Journal of Celtic Studies*, 4 (2004), pp. 219–61

—— '*Tri Dygyngoll Cenedl*: The Development of a Triad', *Studia Celtica*, 37 (2003), pp. 163–82

——, and Christine James (ed. and trans.), *Archwilio Cymru'r Oesoedd Canol: Testunau o Gyfraith Hywel*, Texts and Studies in Medieval Welsh Law, 4 (Seminar Cyfraith Hywel, 2015)

——, and Ceridwen Lloyd-Morgan, 'In the Undergrowth: Llwyn a Pherth and Sexual Deviancy in Medieval Wales', in *Women's Literary Cultures in the Global Middle Ages: Speaking Internationally*, ed. by Kathryn Loveridge, Liz Herbert McAvoy, Sue Niebrzydowski, and Vicki Kay Price (D. S. Brewer, 2022), pp. 261–75

Rodway, Simon, *Dating Medieval Welsh Literature: Evidence from the Verbal System* (CMCS, 2013)

——, and Myriah Williams, '*Bullo .i. bronnced*?: Another Look at Two Obscure Words for Horse Tack in *De raris fabulis*', *CMCS*, 83 (2022), pp. 49–63

Rowland, Jenny, *A Selection of Early Welsh Saga Poems*, MHRA Library of Medieval Welsh Literature, 3 (MHRA, 2014)

Sims-Williams, Patrick, *Buchedd Beuno: The Middle Welsh 'Life' of St Beuno* (Dublin Institute for Advanced Studies, 2018)

—— 'Sandhi *h* after Third-Person Pronouns in Middle Welsh', *Celtica*, 34 (2022), pp. 60–86

Smith, Eleanor, 'Baptism, Kinship, and Incest in *Math uab Mathonwy*', *CMCS*, 88 (2024), pp. 1–19

Smith, Llinos Beverley, 'Fosterage, Adoption and God-parenthood: Ritual and Fictive Kinship in Medieval Wales', *Welsh History Review*, 16.1 (1992), pp. 1–35

—— 'Proofs of Age in Medieval Wales', *Bulletin of the Board of Celtic Studies*, 38 (1991), pp. 134–44

Stacey, Robin Chapman, *Law and the Imagination in Medieval Wales* (University of Pennsylvania Press, 2018)

—— 'Legal Writing in Medieval Wales: Damweiniau I', in *Wales and the Wider World: Welsh History in an International Context*, ed. by T. M. Charles-Edwards and R. J. W. Evans (Shaun Tyas, 2011), pp. 57–85

Stephenson, David, 'The Laws of Court: Past Reality or Present Ideal?', in *The Welsh King and his Court*, ed. by T. M. Charles-Edwards, M. E. Owen, and P. Russell (University of Wales Press, 2000), pp. 400–14

Wade-Evans, A. W., *Welsh Medieval Law, Being a Text of the Laws of Howel the Good* (Oxford University Press, 1909; repr. Scientia Verlag Aalen, 1979)

Walters, Dafydd B., '"A Rodi y Mab a Orucpwyd ar Ueithrin": Bringing up Children in Medieval Wales and Beyond', in *Cyfarwydd Mewn Cyfraith: Studies in Honour of Morfydd E. Owen*, ed. by Sara Elin Roberts, Simon Rodway, and

Alexander Falileyev, Welsh Legal History Society, 17 (Welsh Legal History Society, 2022), pp. 167–78

Wiliam, Aled Rhys, *Llyfr Iorwerth: A Critical Text of the 'Venedotian Code' of Medieval Welsh Law* (University of Wales Press, 1960)

Williams, Ifor, *Pedeir Keinc y Mabinogi* (University of Wales Press, 1951)

Williams, Patricia, *Historical Texts from Medieval Wales*, MHRA Library of Medieval Welsh Literature, 2 (MHRA, 2012)

Williams, Stephen J., *Detholion o'r Hen Gyfreithiau Cymreig* (University of Wales Press, 1938)

——, and J. Enoch Powell, *Llyfr Blegywryd* (University of Wales Press, 1942)

Reference Works and Online Resources

13th-Century Middle Welsh Prose Manuscripts, ed. by G. R. Isaac and Simon Rodway (Aberystwyth University, 2002), doi:10.20391/3abf4ef1-e364-4cce-859d-92bf4035b303

Cyfraith Hywel Website
<http://www.cyfraith-hywel.org.uk>

Dictionary of Welsh Biography (National Library of Wales)
<https://biography.wales>

Digital Bodleian, Oxford, Jesus College MS 57
<https://digital.bodleian.ox.ac.uk/objects/91819125-25f1-4533-9fdd-99a4d1c84491/>

Geiriadur Prifysgol Cymru: A Dictionary of the Welsh Language Online (University of Wales) <https://www.geiriadur.ac.uk/gpc/gpc.html>

National Library of Wales, Digital Exhibitions, Manuscripts, the Middle Ages <https://www.llyfrgell.cymru/darganfod/oriel-ddigidol/llawysgrifau/yr-oesoedd-canol>

Rhyddiaith Gymraeg 1300–1425: Welsh Prose 1300–1425 (Cardiff University) <http://www.rhyddiaithganoloesol.caerdydd.ac.uk/>

The MHRA encourages and promotes advanced study and research in the field of the modern humanities, especially modern European languages and literature, including English, and also cinema. It aims to break down the barriers between scholars working in different disciplines and to maintain the unity of humanistic scholarship. The Association fulfils this purpose through the publication of journals, bibliographies, monographs, critical editions, and the MHRA *Style Guide*, and by making grants in support of research. Membership is open to all who work in the humanities, whether independent or in a university post, and the participation of younger colleagues entering the field is especially welcomed.

ALSO PUBLISHED BY THE ASSOCIATION

Tudor and Stuart Translations • New Translations • European Translations
Critical Texts • Jewelled Tortoise

Legenda

The Annual Bibliography of English Language & Literature

Austrian Studies
Modern Language Review
Portuguese Studies
The Slavonic and East European Review
Working Papers in the Humanities
The Yearbook of English Studies

www.mhra.org.uk

www.ingramcontent.com/pod-product-compliance
Lightning Source LLC
Chambersburg PA
CBHW070939180426
43192CB00039B/2345